Here is a practical guide for anyone in transition, and for those whose work involves managing, guiding or healing others. It provides an innovative approach to living and working with less stress in today's rapidly shifting environment. Through simple exercises, strategies, suggestions, questions, anecdotes, charts and diagrams, Dorri Jacobs shows you how to cope with change and become the architect of your own future.

You'll discover

- The Twelve Keys To A Successful Change
- Why Fear Is An Asset
- The Value Of Crisis

This book will help you to

- Adapt To Modern Technology
- Cope With Unemployment, Job And Career Change
- Manage A Promotion Or A New Boss
- Renegotiate A Relationship
- Overcome Resistance And Create A Climate For Change
- Deal With Separation, Divorce And Widowhood
- Care For a Sick Or Aging Parent
- Enjoy Retirement

CHANGE

Also by Dorri Jacobs
Priorities: How To Stay Young And Keep Growing

CHANGE

HOW TO LIVE WITH, MANAGE, CREATE AND ENJOY IT

Dorri Jacobs, Ed.D.

© 1981 by Dorri Jacobs
All rights reserved. No part of this book may be reproduced or transmitted on any form or by any means without written permission of the author. Printed in the United States of America.

Cover Design: Dale Petry
A publication of Programs On Change
784 Columbus Avenue, New York, N.Y. 10025, Suite 1-C
First Edition   ISBN 0-9606012-0-1
Library of Congress Catalog Card Number: 81-81369

To all those
who willingly shared their stories with me

Contents

Index of Exercises	xi
Acknowledgments	xii

Part One. Direction

Introduction: The Future Is Change		3
Chapter 1.	**Impetus**	8
	Our changing environment • The Victim Syndrome	
Chapter 2.	**The Journey Begins**	23
	Your Path Through The Void • The 12 Keys To Successful Change • The dynamics of change	

Part Two. Interference

Chapter 3.	**The Pull Toward Status Quo**	53
	Simple exercises to increase your motivation	
Chapter 4.	**Understanding Resistance To Change**	64
	5 Causes of resistance and what to do about them	
Chapter 5.	**Make Friends with Fear**	73
	7 Kinds of fear • How to recognize self-defeating behavior • Why fear is an asset	

Part Three. Turnaround and Momentum

Chapter 6.	**Redirecting Negativity**	89
	The energy of fear • How mourning helps	
Chapter 7.	**The Value of Crisis**	97
	Crisis as a changemaker • Appropriate rituals • Crisis and loss	
Chapter 8.	**Ready for Action**	109
	Signs of readiness • The rhythm of change • Procrastination • How to plan	

Part Four. Focus

Chapter 9. Coping with Unemployment — 127
Why we work • Being jobless • Self-fulfilling prophecies • Changing your attitude about money

Chapter 10. Career Transitions — 136
Issues for job and career-changers • Leisure and retirement planning

Chapter 11. Improving and Ending Relationships — 151
Letting go of love • Coping with divorce and bereavement • Techniques for renegotiating a relationship

Chapter 12. Relocating — 171
The long-distance move • Strategies for sharing space or living alone

Chapter 13. The Loss of Health and Mobility — 179
Coping with serious and terminal illness • The impact of aging • Caring for the patient • How to promote wellness

Chapter 14. Wellness at Work — 195
The impact of change in the work world • How to prevent stress

Chapter 15. Helping Others Change — 199
How to become a change agent

Epilogue. Looking Beyond Tomorrow — 202
Appendix. Model For A Training Program On Change — 204
Suggested Readings And Resources — 206
About The Author — 212

Index of Exercises

Chapter 1.	Preliminary Goal List	16
	Self-Check: Your Attitude Toward Change	20
	Gold Stars	20
Chapter 2.	Homecoming	26
	Charting A Change History	35
	Your Reserve Bank	38
	Skyhooks	41
	Priority List	44
	Goal-Digging	47
	Piecework	49
Chapter 3.	Green Flags	56
	Dark Clouds	57
	Red Flags	58
	Embracing Opposites	60
	Tuning In	61
Chapter 4.	Understanding Your Attitude: A Self-Test	71
Chapter 5.	Cover-up Behavior	75
	A Fearful Attitude: A Self-Test	85
Chapter 6.	Worry Beads	91
	Mourning	93
Chapter 7.	Mourning In A Crisis	104
Chapter 8.	Readiness: A Self-Test	112
	The Time Test	115
	Planning For Change	117
Chapter 9.	The Benefits Of Working	127

Acknowledgments

There are many people whose presence nourished, inspired or challenged me and kept me going, whom I wish to thank. Among them are:

All the participants in the workshops on change over the years, whose probing questions led to my refining the material; my clients, from whom I continually learn; Daralee Schulman, Sim Arons and Sabina Green for their wise suggestions upon reading the manuscript, and for their time, which they gave freely; Chris Filner, Director of the YWCA Women's Center, for providing an arena in which to explore my concepts; the Women's Center South, in Pittsburgh, where I presented my first Workshop on Facilitating Change; my friends, Bryna Eill, Miriam Colman and Mildred Fields, and my family, for understanding and putting up with my preoccupation for so many months; Ron Gross, Vince DiGiambattista, Stanley Lowell, Harriet Sussman, Mona Frishman, Sue McMillan, Jerry Slotnick and Siggy Kress, who, among others, expanded my vision; Dr. Leon Zussman, in memoriam, for his continued professional support during the early stages of this project; Ruth Shapiro, for being a loving role model; Olga Scheirr, for her compassion and perspective as an artist; Carolee Berg, Joan Keochakian, Sister Patrice Murphy, Anne Quirk, Retirement Advisors, Inc., Susan J. Jeffers, Ph.D. and Liz Jacobs for their help; and everyone else who energized, cajoled and encouraged me to complete this project, because their collective spirit made it possible.

Above all, a special thank-you to Daralee Schulman, for her endless patience and support.

Part One: Direction

Introduction: The Future Is Change

Collectively, we possess the potential brain power and human resources to solve many of the social and economic problems existing in the world today. If it seems to us that changes are required, we certainly are capable of making them. However, this is not always feasible. The ills of our society are complex. We need visionaries who will direct their energy toward projects implemented on a grand scale.

Instead of addressing ourselves now to this rather momentous task, I suggest that we draw our attention inward. A smaller, more personal focus will make dealing with change in a broader scope possible later. But can we wholeheartedly accept the changes that beset us almost daily and manage them reasonably well? Individually, do we truly understand how to make change happen?

Unfortunately, very few of us can do this adequately. The average person goes through life with only a limited perception of *the process* pursued in reaching goals. Dreams die or are attained somewhat haphazardly. Growth and change occur with much less conscious participation on the part of an individual than he or she might prefer, or than is really possible.

This book was designed to help make what is ordinarily intangible more tangible so that you are much more aware of yourself changing *as* it is happening.

To facilitate this, we will talk about things you might not normally discuss. Although the approach may seem overly simplistic at first glance, this is deceptive. Bringing deeper feelings and nonverbal ways of being that you might initially ignore to the surface so they are accessible is not a simple matter. We are demystifying change, pulling it out into the open and looking at how and when it flourishes. This will help you to monitor your own growth process. Eventually, you will be able to sense the connection between yourself and the universe in terms of movement, energy, direction and rhythm.

This book serves as a guide to help you help yourself. It gives you a language and the tools to sort out any confusion you may feel about managing or facilitating change. It will show you how to ask the kind of questions that focus your thinking and foster creative solutions. Step by step, it will also show you how to take positive action, accelerate your progress and evaluate the results. Your new perspective will make you more empathetic to others. This will be useful in work that involves supervising, guiding or healing.

What is described here is a fluid process, rather than a formula. The content is based upon research conducted for over five years, personal experiences and a system for change which has been tested by hundreds of people and found very effective. Ranging in age from eighteen to seventy years, they were private clients of mine in workshops, seminars and counseling. Their occupations included business executives, secretaries, housewives, teachers, artists, musicians, postal clerks, ex-seminary students, accountants, lawyers, and computer programmers. Most were in periods of critical transition and felt confused or discouraged. Each participant in the program was able to see his or her own progress within a short time. They became clearer about their future directions, and developed an increasing awareness of where they were today, where they were headed and how to get there most effectively. Because alternatives appeared, they felt encouraged.

Like them, you can clarify your direction and expand possible options. Like them, you can effect whatever changes are necessary to improve your life.

Follow at your own individual pace. Although the program is presented here in a logical progression, if you cannot handle one part or think it is too heavy, go back to it later when it seems more appropriate. Please don't expect overnight success with no setbacks. That would be unrealistic. You'll need patience and the ability to laugh at yourself as well as cry. Humor is a powerful ally which takes the edge off fear.

Fear is a vital part of the process. Instead of eliminating it, you'll learn how to make fear an asset.

I know from personal experience just how scary changemaking is. I always wanted more adventure, but like most people I took only calculated risks. To insure a supposedly secure economic future, I held onto an intellectually and emotionally unsatisfying job. My days were predictable and uninteresting, my self-respect low. The price I paid was feeling bored, unchallenged and trapped, with talents and energy largely unused.

When my frustration finally became more important than any anxiety about the future, I made up my mind. At age thirty-nine, feeling ready to leave what was familiar and carve out a new life, I handed in my resignation. In one fell swoop I changed my career, finances, daily environment, self-image and lifestyle. The territory was uncharted and I had no map. With no handles other than myself and a very limited savings account, I plunged into the unknown. Although I had no set structure or means of income, my direction was quite clear, I would continue the work I'd begun several years earlier—on a freelance basis.

It all fell into place rather quickly. My first book, *Priorities* was published by Franklin Watts. Under the auspices of my firm, Programs On Change, I presented workshops, lectures and seminars for individuals, groups and industry on managing change, and increased my private counseling practice. My reputation grew. I was frequently consulted as a specialist on the subject of change. The media interviewed me. I began to savor the exhilaration of a success I had created.

Today, anxiety no longer handicaps me and my mood is generally optimistic. Having evolved a lifestyle that gives me great personal satisfaction, I've become a role model for others to follow.

What gave me the impetus, courage and self-assurance

to take that first scary step of leaving my job was the training program I had developed several years earlier. By the time I actually left, I was so immersed in this work that the techniques for successful changemaking were like second nature to me. Because I believed that it was possible and also possessed the necessary tools, I was able to reshape the texture and focus of my life.

Originally searching for ways to help my clients overcome their blocks and fears, I developed a theory. Its premise is that people in a crisis situation, out of a survival instinct, teach themselves to cope. These strategies can be applied by choice later when a change is sought. To explore this further, I began interviewing. My subjects were those who had, in their own opinion, so successfully weathered a crisis and the unexpected changes it brought that they emerged stronger. The raw material from these interviews evolved into the program I created for anyone in transition. Its content was updated regularly, with the material tested and new ideas incorporated. This book actually includes far more techniques than the early workshops.

Part 1 shows you how, through simple diagrams, exercises and explanations, to develop a fresh attitude toward change and to build the necessary resources. It also discusses how to facilitate any kind of change.

Part 2 explains why people resist change as well as common ways in which they prevent themselves from getting ahead. It provides simple strategies for overcoming such reluctance, including how to make fear an asset.

Part 3 presents practical techniques for putting your plans into action. It explores the value of crisis and gives you additional tools for initiating and managing change.

Part 4 shows you how to apply the concepts in this book to situations that occur every day. It discusses strategies for coping with change in:

- your job or career
- your lifestyle
- your relationships
- your work or home environments

- your financial status
- your health

The focus is on capsuled life histories of people who have successfully coped with change. The people whose stories are presented here will probably remind you of yourself, your colleagues, family and friends. This section also gives suggestions for helping others change. Lastly, it gives you a glimpse of the future.

From its inception to the early stages of writing, to its publication, this book has acted as a powerful change agent in my life. It was as though its energy pushed, pulled, prodded and propelled me at a very rapid speed toward new areas of personal and professional growth. You can capitalize on the same energy, using it to thrust you in a direction of your own choosing.

We have begun what will most likely prove to be a very exciting journey. Seize this remarkable opportunity for self-renewal. Accept the uncertainties that lie ahead because they will lead you to greater satisfaction.

I offer you both the challenge and the hope for a fuller, more daring life as *you* wish to live it.

Chapter 1: Impetus

Facing a Changing World

The last fifty years have been mind-boggling in terms of social, political, economic and technological change. So much has transpired in such a short period of time that we are still in shock.

Before any of us had quite recovered from the sexual revolution and greater availability of birth control, test tube babies were spawned. The jet age brought moon landings, travel in space and solar energy. While heart transplants and microsurgery saved lives, several renowned political and creative leaders were assassinated. Complacently, we watched the Vietnam War on television. Watergate and Abscam scandals rocked the government. It seemed as though all the values which we had cherished for so long had somehow vanished. Then fifty-two Americans were held hostage for more than a year.

It is certainly easy to become frustrated, disillusioned or frightened in today's world. The latest news bulletins constantly test our adaptability to new situations. Whether it is international affairs, the oil crisis, a recent election, the economy, a plane crash, transportation strike or drought, a continuous whirlwind of events with far-reaching impact shifts your focus away from smaller, more personal issues.

In a society where neither fatal diseases, manmade nor natural disasters are fully under our control (in spite of our ability to conquer outer space), where your bodily safety may be threatened at any moment by random and often violent crime, of course you feel off-balance. Something new is always happening to undermine your equilibrium—

at work, among your circle of friends, in your neighborhood or on the national scene.

Change is an inevitable part of modern society. Transition is now the norm. An increasing divorce rate, single parenthood, later retirement and extended leisure have created brave new lifestyles with apparently unlimited options. Unclear and overlapping roles, expendable values and varying standards for behavior make the old ways of thinking, relating and planning obsolete. You are faced with repeated readjustments as a result of economic recession, widespread unemployment, modern technology, business expansion, greater advancement of women and minorities and the possibility of starting a second or perhaps a third career. Everything is in such a perpetual state of flux that by the time you even begin to adjust, the situation you're in is already different. Even our vocabulary reflects this: women's movement, crisis center, career-pathing, life-planning, pre-retirement, displaced homemaker, employee turnover, organizational development, new wave and generation gap.

Can you keep in step? Unless you are able to adapt to today's changing world, you will find yourself out of sync, antideluvian, without control of your life.

How well do you cope with the unexpected? Over the years, you have probably faced countless disappointments and crises, each demanding new resources, responsibilities and means of coping. Tomorrow may bring still more changes to challenge you. Will you be up to them?

Think of the unexpected events you've recently experienced. Here are a few examples.

- A new boss replaces the one who appreciated all your efforts.
- Your company is going out of business.
- The entire basement is flooded.
- Your child falls seriously ill and must be hospitalized.
- A drunken driver races through an intersection and demolishes the parked family car.

What has been your pattern of behavior in such situations? How did you manage?

Change need not be only traumatic or problematic. Getting engaged, winning the lottery, completing a degree or getting a promotion are usually considered positive events in a person's life. But how a person responds to a new situation is an individual matter.

People react to change in different ways. Some people seem to thrive on it. If you are like them, you:

- find that change makes your life more interesting
- seek its challenge
- rise to the occasion
- use it to actualize your potential
- feel energized
- use it to find new solutions to difficult problems
- find that change stimulates you
- gain greater confidence through coping with change

Others are just the opposite. They don't like change at all. Because any change is very upsetting to them, they much prefer the status quo. If a change throws you off balance, you may:

- ignore it, pretending that it doesn't exist
- withdraw from the world for a while in order to get back your equilibrium
- develop physical symptoms of stress: severe back or muscle tension and pain, chest congestion, nausea, cramps, even ulcers and heart disease
- feel inadequate and unprepared, full of self-doubt
- get defensive in situations you feel you cannot handle
- become angry or depressed

Which of these responses is most like yours?

Just how comfortable with change are you? How well do you cope?

Take Charge of Your Life

I believe that we all have the power and intelligence to improve the quality of our lives. Instead of merely reacting to events as if we had no control over them at all, each of us can live with a minimum of stress in a rapidly changing world. Life is to be experienced fully, not insulated against. The fear of being irrevocably hurt, the need for security does not have to mean confining yourself to a safe but dull existence where dreams of change are doomed by default.

Not only can you learn to adapt to changes you never sought, but you can also develop the confidence, resources and skills to actively create the kind of future you want. At this very moment, begin by taking charge of your own destiny.

The first thing to do is something you've already begun—and that is reading this book. It provides you with a path to follow. Instead of attempting to do everything at once to change your life, be a bit more humble. Concentrate on the smaller issues at first. The larger ones of course will involve more effort.

In the next few weeks, you will notice many small yet significant changes. Your view of what seems possible will keep expanding. How long it takes for you to accomplish the things you want will depend upon just how major a change each one represents.

When you adopt a more positive attitude, almost anything is within your reach. Recapture your sense of adventure so that you are free to take greater risks more comfortably. Whether you're interested in altering your strategies at work, renegotiating a relationship, changing your job, directing your energies toward modifying organizational systems or the government, the approaches are practically identical. Regardless of the specific change sought, your attitude and behavior in bringing it about is crucial.

Let's look at your track record for a minute. How do you rate yourself in terms of successfully achieving your goals? To answer this, think of a change that you eagerly anticipated, initiated or planned for, such as:
- a new home
- a promotion
- a challenging job
- marriage
- a baby

Consider also those ventures about which you had quite mixed emotions, as for instance:
- losing weight
- subletting your apartment
- finding a roommate
- going back to school
- taking a year off to travel or write
- starting a business
- ending a long-term relationship

What happened when you decided to improve your situation? In spite of occasional setbacks, could you proceed full steam ahead?

Of course no one has complete personal freedom. Life deals strange twists of fate which keep us from perpetual bliss. It would be unrealistic to expect otherwise. But start to believe that it is possible to shape your own future as you see fit.

Instead of drifting rather aimlessly over the years, you have the power to follow a set course that *you* choose. I'm suggesting that you start now to clarify what you want and go after it with a fierce determination balanced only by a degree of flexibility and the ability to cope with whatever circumstances arise. Feel the upheaval of change but do not allow it to upset you. Life is more meaningful when you know you are headed in a direction largely of your own making yet can also adapt quite readily to the unexpected without losing your optimism.

Pause for a second. Does this picture sound too good to be true, too far removed from your everyday reality for you to accept? Whether it is a job that you find too boring or a relationship which causes you unhappiness, unless some viable alternatives magically appear, the situation may seem hopeless. Certainly you'd like to have things different than they are. But since you're not doing anything to make this happen and the prospect of initiating even one change presently stymies you, how is it going to occur?

Getting your life the way you want it to be can be simpler than you might at first think. If you're willing to devote a minimum of an hour a day or at least several hours a week and do the necessary work, you can accomplish *almost* anything you want. The *almost* is added merely as a check against grandiose, totally unrealistic dreams. *You can make anything happen.* After all, you are the architect of your own future.

I strongly believe that we *do* have choices.

So take an active role. Decide that you definitely want a better life. Take the responsibility for what happens to you.

I'm going to show you exactly how to do this, step by step.

Some Definitions

In order to proceed, you'll need to know more about change, especially how it occurs and how it is generally experienced emotionally.

What is change?

Change is an evolution, an opening and unfolding of your inner self as you reach toward specific goals or states of being for which you've been striving. It is a period of *movement*, involving activities, alternatives, decisions and survival rather than being passive, inert, feeling stuck, impotent or lifeless.

This movement is not always apparent to others, or even to you. But that does not mean that you are not changing. Give yourself time and you will start to see a difference.

There are four ways in which you can change:

- in the way you think
- in what you feel
- in how you behave—in your general demeanor
- in what you do—in the actions you take

Doing and behaving are often a direct result of thinking and feeling.

What does this mean? How does change happen?

You change in a continuous cycle. The parameters of

thinking, feeling, behaving and action overlap. When you feel differently, you will probably be motivated to take some action. This action undoubtedly has repercussions. Their impact acts as a stimulus for a change in your attitude. A changed attitude causes you to take another action, and so on. Here is a visual explanation of this cycle:

The Way We Change

change in thinking → **change in behavior**

You realize that you need and want more people in your life and had better do something to make this happen. ↑

You are more friendly and outgoing with others.

↑ ↓

change in feeling ← **change in action**

You become more self-confident and less shy.

You invite friends over more often. Then they invite you and your social calendar becomes filled.

The impetus for change can be external or internal. An example of the former is when your company goes bankrupt and you subsequently lose your job. An external event has been imposed upon you, altering your self-image and perspective, forcing you into rethinking possible directions to take. It is much easier to make a change when it originates from the inside. In the diagram's example, you are aware of a need and as a result reach out to others. When a change is motivated by your emotions and will, because you have a much more secure base from which to move, it is more likely to be permanent.

How is change usually experienced?

When you let go of a familiar self-image, shed old selves and ideas, the experience can be unsettling. Such metamorphosis is neither quick nor painless. Making any change involves facing the fear, ambivalence and uncertainty of what is to come. Because you are giving up so much, because the future is still unclear, because neither you nor your life will ever be quite the same again once you have taken the first steps toward changing, you may experience an unbearable sense of loss. This is mainly a temporary loss of self. (Such feelings are explored more deeply in Part 2.)

Why do you feel this way when you attempt a change?

The reason that you are often uncomfortable is that the familiar framework of your life which lent structure and support is gone. This puts you in a different space with no known direction, rules or boundaries. With few apparent resources upon which to rely, you may feel disoriented, fearful, anxious or inadequate. No longer the YOU you once were and not being sure yet just who you are, for a time it is almost as though you ceased to exist.

It isn't necessary to flounder any more because of these feelings. There are things you can do to feel more in control.

A New Direction

You need somewhere to start, something to look forward to. This will give you a focus and direction.

Take a look at your life today. Do you know yourself well enough to state what is really important to you? Examine more than one aspect of your life: your job, professional field, income, appearance, attitude, habits, friends, lovelife or living space. Where is there room for improvement? With what are you dissatisfied? Why? What is not quite right?

Keeping your answers to these questions in mind, now decide what changes you want to make. Then start to list them.

We will call these changes *your preliminary goals*. Don't think about how fitting they may be a week or a year from now. You cannot possibly know now what you will feel or want tomorrow. No one can. Instead of taking the position that whatever you list must be exactly right today and forever, draw up your goals with an eye toward fluidity of content. Don't be concerned either with feasibility or with the consequences of reaching them. Keep your options open. For now, assume that you can get whatever training, money or time you might need to accomplish them.

Here is a sample list.

Preliminary Goals

1. Lose weight
2. Sublet my apartment
3. Move to a larger apartment
4. Go back to college
5. Complete my degree
6. Be more open and friendly
7. Become more confident
8. Get to work on time
9. Be more organized
10. Start a relationship that might lead to marriage

You'll notice that these goals are varied in scope and in the time it will take to reach them. Once there are between five to ten items on your Preliminary Goal list, you'll be off to a good start. If it is too soon for you to know what you want changed, your first goal would be to devote a period of time to thinking about your life and what you want. Begin with wherever you are now, not with where you think you *should* be. This allows you to pinpoint your goals as you are ready.

A positive attitude is a primary resource which will help you to make the changes you want. Staying optimistic depends upon believing in your power to effect change and build a more rewarding lifestyle. Let's look at this now.

Your Belief System

What is your belief system?
To find out, ask yourself the following two questions.
- Do I believe in my own ability to effect change?
- Can I influence and control the direction of my life?

Say them aloud this time as positive statements rather than questions. Listen to your tone of voice and sense of conviction as you speak.

"I believe in my own ability to effect change."
"I can influence and control the direction of my life."

What do you hear? Do your statements sound as though you sincerely mean them? Do the words ring true?

The Victim Syndrome

If you could not make these two statements with assurance, if self-doubt crept into your voice, perhaps you are suffering from the Victim Syndrome. Victims view the world from a perspective of helplessness. The following is an exaggeration of this:

They often feel impotent, an unfortunate outcome of seeing themselves as victims. Believing that life just happens *to* them, and that the power to live any differently is out of their hands, they act as though they have no freedom of choice. Preferring passivity, they take no initiative. Events control them. They tell themselves that everyone else has more education or training, faith, love, funds or optimism than they, so they cannot possibly be expected to do anything to change their circumstances. Feeling too old, young, weary, discouraged, overqualified or untrained, they are absolutely sure that no other way of surviving is possible. This is just the way things are. Anything else would be a pipe dream. Tossed hither and yon by others' needs, expectations and demands, or kept in stasis by fear and insecurity, they resign themselves to a life without too many risks. Expressions like "My husband/wife won't let me," "I can't," "Yes, but...," "If only...," or "That's impossible for me" crop up often in their conversation. Rather than being overly realistic, they are generally ruled by pessimism or fatalism.

Does this description fit you in any way?

Are you at all caught in the Victim Syndrome?

If you feel like a victim of circumstance, with no options open to you, your lot is not a happy one. Such a defeated attitude is fairly common. But don't despair. Help is at hand. That is what this book is about—turning such a negative outlook around.

If you were brought up in the "me" generation, taught that anything was possible, such blind optimism is too extreme. It often produces disillusionment and the giving up on dreams. Please don't think that a middle position is any better—and thus continually lower your expectations to fit the moment. Here, you may end up with a life that's mediocre.

You don't have to be a victim, overly optimistic or too passive. There is a solution. You'll be satisfied about the way you are living—when you start to make choices and plan changes. Change can be accomplished without great discomfort, without disruption, without your days full of obstacles to be overcome. To be more in charge of your life, work on improving your attitude.

A Positive Attitude

To insure a greater chance for success in future endeavors, develop an appropriate attitude toward change. You'll get ahead more smoothly with these qualities: tenacity, commitment, faith, a sense of responsibility, self-awareness, self-acceptance, self-love, patience, singlemindedness of purpose, flexibility, assertiveness and courage.

Tenacity. Nothing really important can be accomplished overnight. So stick to whatever you are doing. Don't be a quitter. Try not to get discouraged and give up at the first setback or sign of a problem.

Commitment. Make a deep commitment to yourself. Tell yourself that you are important. What you feel and wish *does* count.

Faith. Believe in your ability to get what you want. Be optimistic and trust in the future. You do not have to fully believe in my telling you that you can create change. Just take it on faith for the moment.

A Sense of Responsibility. Take responsibility for yourself and for whatever you feel. Stop hoping that something or someone will come along and save you with money, a perfect job, lover or magical solution to your troubles. Only you have the power to make your life work.

Self-Awareness, Self-Acceptance and Self-Love. Try not to compare yourself to anyone else or to your ideal. Know what you feel. Accept wherever you are at this moment. Understand that if you move diligently at your own pace, in time you'll be far beyond this point.

Patience. Trust that what you want will be achieved gradually. Eventually, your journey will seem less fraught with hardships. Impatience doesn't really speed up the process.

Singlemindedness of Purpose. Stay on target. Writing serves as a means of pulling a jumble of thoughts together and making them more tangible than when they floated around in your head. So, if you have the time and the interest, keep a Change Notebook. Jot down your thoughts, feelings, questions, answers, goals, dreams, activities, others' suggestions. The book should be small enough to fit into your pocket or purse so that you can carry it with you. Your notes will help you to organize, clarify, focus, record and evaluate any progress you do make. Keep your goals in mind as you go through daily routines. Agree to do the work involved in reaching them. Allow ample time for rethinking future plans. Don't be easily swayed by others.

Flexibility. Staying on track does not mean to hit your head against a brick wall. A certain degree of flexibility is surely necessary. Take a different tack when it seems practical.

Assertiveness. Take an assertive stance. Give yourself the right to make changes in your life, to be selfish, to take the time to go after what you want.

Courage. Making any major change requires bravery. When you act in spite of your fear, you are being brave. So be sure to acknowledge your courage. If you weren't at all afraid, you wouldn't truly be brave.

What is your attitude toward change?

Rate yourself from 0 to 10 on the qualities I just mentioned. Use the lowest number for those qualities *least* like you, and the highest number for those qualities *most* like you. No one has a totally appropriate attitude, so don't despair if you find yourself rather low in many categories. This exercise just shows you where to begin working.

Self-Check: Your Attitude Toward Change

0 = least like me
10 = most like me

qualities	0 1 2 3 4 5 6 7 8 9 10
tenacity	
commitment	
faith	
sense of responsibility	
self-awareness	
self-acceptance	
self-love	
patience	
singlemindedness of purpose	
flexibility	
assertiveness	
courage	

If you are feeling a little insecure at this moment, after looking at your attitude, there is something you can do to remedy your state of mind.

Gold Stars

Even though you don't need the gold stars that teachers in grade school gave you when you did something right, you still need some recognition for your efforts. You don't need someone else to do it, because you can give such praise to yourself.

It is crucial for your future successes that you learn to give yourself credit even for very small achievements, regardless of how trivial they may seem. Be sure to take a bow for what you've attempted, even if it did not turn out exactly as you had hoped. Keep a running list. Put on it whatever you've done so far. Get used to writing down these pats on the back and considering them as valid actions on the road to change. This will give you a sense of greater accomplishment and help you feel so much more secure in the future about any changemaking you do.

Here is a sample list to get you started. Continue it on your own.

Gold Stars

1. I started to think about making changes in my life.
2. I bought this book.
3. I am reading it seriously.
4. I am keeping a Change Notebook and devoting several hours each week to working on my life.
5. I've admitted that I am somewhat dissatisfied with my life.
6. I've picked out some specific things I want to change.
7. I've written them down as Preliminary Goals.
8. I examined my belief system.
9. I checked my attitude toward change and found out where I need to focus.
10. I am attempting to do something about my situation, even if I don't yet really believe that it is possible.
11. I am starting to make a list of actions I've taken, so as to give myself credit and boost my confidence. I know that this will help me to make further changes.

The purpose of this list is to give you greater assurance and to prove to you that you've already progressed. Be proud of yourself!

Change: An Ongoing Process

Changemaking is not magical, mystical or difficult. In general, you'll be taking many forward steps, although sometimes it will appear as though nothing is happening, you are stagnating or even reversing direction.

But relax. Changemaking is an ongoing process involving motion in many directions as well as periods of inactivity. You need not be "doing" something actively all of the time. Even if you find them very painful, please don't discount the long stretches of quiet between activity. These periods are creative rests and very constructive. They give you the space to regather the energy you spent in the search for a better life, recover from the exhaustion of confronting your feelings, and dream. You are certainly not being passive in such times, only preparing yourself for future action.

Although not without stress, living with change can be pleasurable, exciting and challenging. In the following chapter, you'll continue the work you've just started by exploring the concepts, learning the skills and practicing the exercises to help you cope more efficiently with a changing world and to make the rest of your life more rewarding.

Chapter 2: The Journey Begins

Facing The Void

If until now you tried to maintain the status quo, or if the goal you've decided upon represents a major change, you're probably feeling rather insecure. Impatience to get to your destination is a common reaction. Don't be surprised if most of your self-confidence disappears. It's hard to proceed with assurance when the future looms menacingly as a shapeless, dark and empty void.

Of course you feel uneasy. The prospect of facing this void is like being adrift at sea. Imagine yourself trying to steer a small boat with no oars, sail or motor. Obstacles appear at every turn, threatening your safety. You're unclear about where you've come from and where you're headed. Heavy winds and a fierce current toss you unmercifully about. Land is nowhere in sight. You cannot locate a safe harbor or familiar landmark by which to plot a course. If only someone would save you!

But you can save yourself. You'll feel much better about the future by putting it into proper perspective. Here's what to do:

• Realize that you are now in transition, somewhere between the known and familiar and the unknown and unfamiliar. The sooner you can accept being in this space, the more comfortable you will feel about change. Welcome to the void!

• You may feel as though you are floating aimlessly with no direction at all. However, you are actually on a path, headed toward a new destination you have chosen. The path leads to your successfully executing a specific change, namely, one of the goals selected from your Preliminary Goals List.

- Consider where you were before you were in transition. Give your present uncertainty more substance by stating what it is that you are leaving: a marriage, a job, being single, being fat.
- Give your goal a place in time. Estimate how long it will take you to reach your goal, in weeks, months, or perhaps even years.

To make it seem like more of a reality, start talking about the change you are making, with these points in mind. For instance, if you are presently unemployed, you might say:

"I am between jobs. My last position was as a manager in a pharmaceutical firm. I left because the company relocated to Texas and I didn't want to move. Now I am exploring other job options. I have enough money for several months, so I don't have to panic and grab the first opportunity that comes along unless I feel sure it is right. I expect to have a new job in one to four months."

I'd like to pose a major question now: How will I get to my destination? I can reassure you that you will, with the assistance of the program in this book—the Changemaking techniques.

Your answers should have made the void seem less threatening. Take a look at how we have just restructured it:

Your Path Through the Void

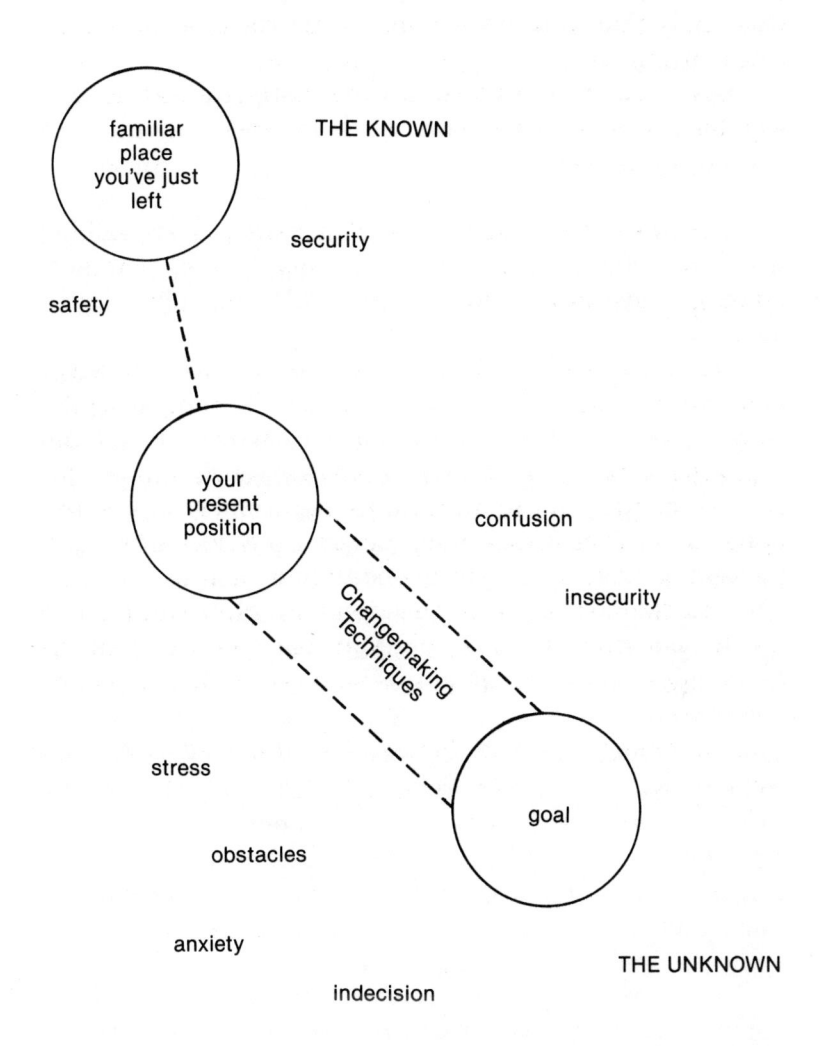

THE KNOWN

familiar place you've just left

security

safety

your present position

confusion

insecurity

Changemaking Techniques

stress

goal

obstacles

anxiety

THE UNKNOWN

indecision

The Journey Begins 25

Homecoming

To reduce any anxiety about the future which you may still harbor, begin to explore and reconnect to your past. Within it are the seeds of change.

The physical and emotional environment in which you were raised, your educational, social, religious, economic and cultural background, your prior experience and relationships greatly influenced your present feelings, values and decisions. On a psychic level, the past, present and future are a part of you at each moment, intertwined in your being, a source of enormous energy. So try not to sever yourself from your roots by denying their impact. If you do, you'll only find yourself bound more tightly, unable to shift gears and mobilize yourself for an independent existence.

This is precisely what happened to one of my clients when he jumped from the theological to the secular world. When Matthew left the priesthood, he considered the years spent there wasted. So Matthew concentrated on forgetting them. He never told his family about his present life, assuming that they would never understand or approve of his decision. This created problems. At age twenty-five, when he first came to my workshop, Matthew felt isolated, unconnected to other people, ill at ease with them, unable to understand their feelings or clearly communicate his own. After several months of hard work, Matthew had dramatically changed his perspective. "I'm looking forward to being with my parents this Christmas, for the first time in years. I always used to feel like an outsider. Now I see that my folks are really like everyone else—and so am I. I feel like I belong. I told my father about my life, and how important self-awareness is to me. He seems pretty understanding. I'm glad I'm going home."

Don't view the past as proof of your failures and shortcomings, as Matthew did at first. See if you can begin to come to terms with your heritage. Which of your family's expectations of life have you adopted? What legacy was left to you—of attitudes, ethics, lifestyle and dreams?

Think about how you've changed since you grew up and

moved out either physically or psychologically. Which ideas and values did you reject? Why?

It's time to have a homecoming. Return home, either in actuality, as Matthew will this Christmas, or in your imagination. Look for the connections between your past experiences, present circumstances and future dreams. When you go back, try to have a fresh perspective. Be open to the possibility that the members of your family may also have changed, as you have. Even though you don't expect their unconditional approval, at least allow yourself to receive your parents' acceptance of your growth. You may find unexpected support here for your future dreams. So be sure not to shut off communication unless you're certain that any mutuality is impossible.

You've just switched from looking toward tomorrow to examining things that are part of yesterday, hurtling tens of years in your mind's eye in a matter of minutes. Change is thus facilitated, by connecting memories with dreams of the future.

When you are not leaping through time, you may experience a sensation of floating in space, ungrounded. Such rootlessness can make you even more uneasy, unless you find the means of creating order in what feels like chaos. The way to do this is to find something to hold onto, tools that will help you to take charge of your life even when you feel so vulnerable.

You don't have to go looking very far for these tools, because they are very much a part of you. That's why I will refer to them as your resources for change. I've named these resources the Twelve Keys to Change. They are:

1. Your Past Changes
2. Your Strengths For Coping With Change
3. Your Fantasy of Success—and Failure
4. Your Priorities
5. Your Goals
6. Your Motivation For Change
7. Your Fear and Resistance To Change
8. Time For Mourning Your Loss

9. Support For The Change
10. Timing And Readiness
11. A Plan
12. Action

The Twelve Keys To Change

Let's look at them individually. After a brief explanation, we'll explore them in more depth.

1. *Your Past Changes.* You already have a long record of success in making changes. Yes, you really do! Think about it: hundreds of times over the years, you coped with new situations, made decisions, altered your behavior, attitude or lifestyle in some significant way. Even if you are not especially pleased with the manner in which you handled yourself, regardless of how well or badly you coped at the time, you survived. Your being here today is proof of this.

Identifying several significant changes made over the years will help you to face future changes with much greater confidence.

2. *Your Strengths For Coping With Change.* Although you may attribute the success of each significant change made in your life to the support or suggestions of others, this is not the whole picture. Even though other people did assist you, giving them all the credit overlooks the importance of your own role. Unless you were open to receiving whatever support was offered, it would have made little impact.

To clarify your strengths for coping with change, we will examine your personal history from a different perspective than that to which you are accustomed. The focus will be on your own inner resources rather than on others' abilities, on what got you through each difficult period of change.

3. *Fantasy of Success—And Failure.* In moments of optimism, you cheerfully daydream about what you would like to happen. These reveries bring relief from the terrible fates you envision when you're feeling unsure. Allow your

imagination to swing to both extremes. Such flights of fancy can be useful. If appropriately channelled, they will facilitate any of the changes you want.

4. *Your Priorities.* Your priorities can be identified by looking at whatever you consider very important in life. They are based upon a personal philosophy: a combination of your values, attitudes and feelings.

It is important to clarify the things that matter to you. Otherwise you may ignore them or take them for granted when thinking about future plans. Remember that no change will please you unless it originates from and is compatible with your priorities.

5. *Your Goals.* Goals are a target for which you are headed. Based upon your priorities, they are clearly defined and fairly simple, very specific manageable tasks which you can surely accomplish within a particular period of time.

Without clear goals, change can be chaotic.

6. *Your Motivation For Change.* Motivation is the pull forward *toward* the change, your reasons for going ahead. Here is energy for mobilizing yourself into positive activity.

When your desire for a change is stronger than your reluctance to make it, you are in a good position to proceed.

7. *Your Fear And Resistance To Change.* There are counter-forces that pull you away from making a change. Because they appear to prevent you from taking action, you may consider them in direct opposition to whatever is motivating you.

However, there is another way to look at this. Fear is actually a valuable asset. Like your motivation, it has considerable energy which can be utilized in a positive way so that it facilitates change.

8. *Time For Mourning Your Loss.* Mourning is usually associated with death and loss. A change is like a death as it signifies the end of something you found meaningful. At this time, mourning is appropriate.

To mourn, you must understand the specific loss being faced, acknowledge your loss by a period of grieving, and then let go emotionally of this part of your life or way of behaving.

9. *Support For The Change.* Support is anything which encourages you to make the change. It can be from others who are sympathetic to your dreams, from the environment in which you live and work, or from *yourself.*

A change will come less painfully and more easily when you have sufficient support.

10. *Timing And Readiness.* There is an appropriate moment to make a change. To decide this, you must consider which pace you find most comfortable and how you really feel about this step. Also useful is the ability to flow with the environment. Such sensitivity can be learned.

Awareness of your timing and readiness for a new venture will help you to move ahead more smoothly, and with less stress.

11. *A Plan.* A plan is like a map of what to do or how to proceed. It requires the ability to organize, select and make decisions about what steps to follow.

Making a plan gives you relief from the confusion and ambiguity of change.

12. *Action.* Action implies that you are seizing opportunities and generating the kind of involvements that bring you closer to a better way of life—instead of being passive and doing nothing.

It is important that you begin to identify and take credit for what is accomplished on the way toward each goal. A change occurs through your completing a long series of small, simple actions.

Although I have just presented them in a definite sequence, changemaking does not usually occur so systematically. These Twelve Keys tend to float in and out of focus, shift their places and merge. Boundaries become unclear. You may be concentrating with great effort on one area when another suddenly seems more important.

The Dynamics of Change

Change involves motion and dynamics: bursts of energy, abrupt stops, enormous leaps, shifts of direction, a slow but steady forward thrust.

Think of changemaking as a dance which you choreograph. Its sequences are interrelated and overlapping, requiring your sensitive orchestration. Sometimes you'll have difficulty in feeling grounded, because the motion takes over and carries you along. At other times you'll lose your perspective and wonder in what direction you're going.

Try to sense the flow of movement in your life: the speed, direction and focus of the dance of years. Notice how you keep the momentum going. What happens when you hit an obstruction? Are you suddenly thrown off-balance, reeling, knocked down and dizzy, or do you fly around it?

To help you to get a sense of the interrelationship of the Twelve Keys and to see change as an ongoing flowing process, I have included several simple drawings. As we do not all perceive the world in the same manner, neither do we learn through the same methods. Some people rely upon words and reason, while others prefer pictures and nonverbal modalities. These diagrams depict a concept, namely, the process of change, by appealing to the less rational, more intuitive and creative parts of your brain.

Use them to experience the continuous motion of the Twelve Keys. The darker-ringed circle in each cluster is your starting point. Assume that none of the circles is ever stationary. Follow the direction of the arrows. Instead of trying to analyze with your head, merely feel kinesthetically. Imagine a mobile with segments blowing in the wind, first going in one direction, then in another. The patterns are forever rearranging themselves.

Get an overview of The Twelve Keys to Change on an intuitive level. Then we will discuss the material they represent.

32 *Change*

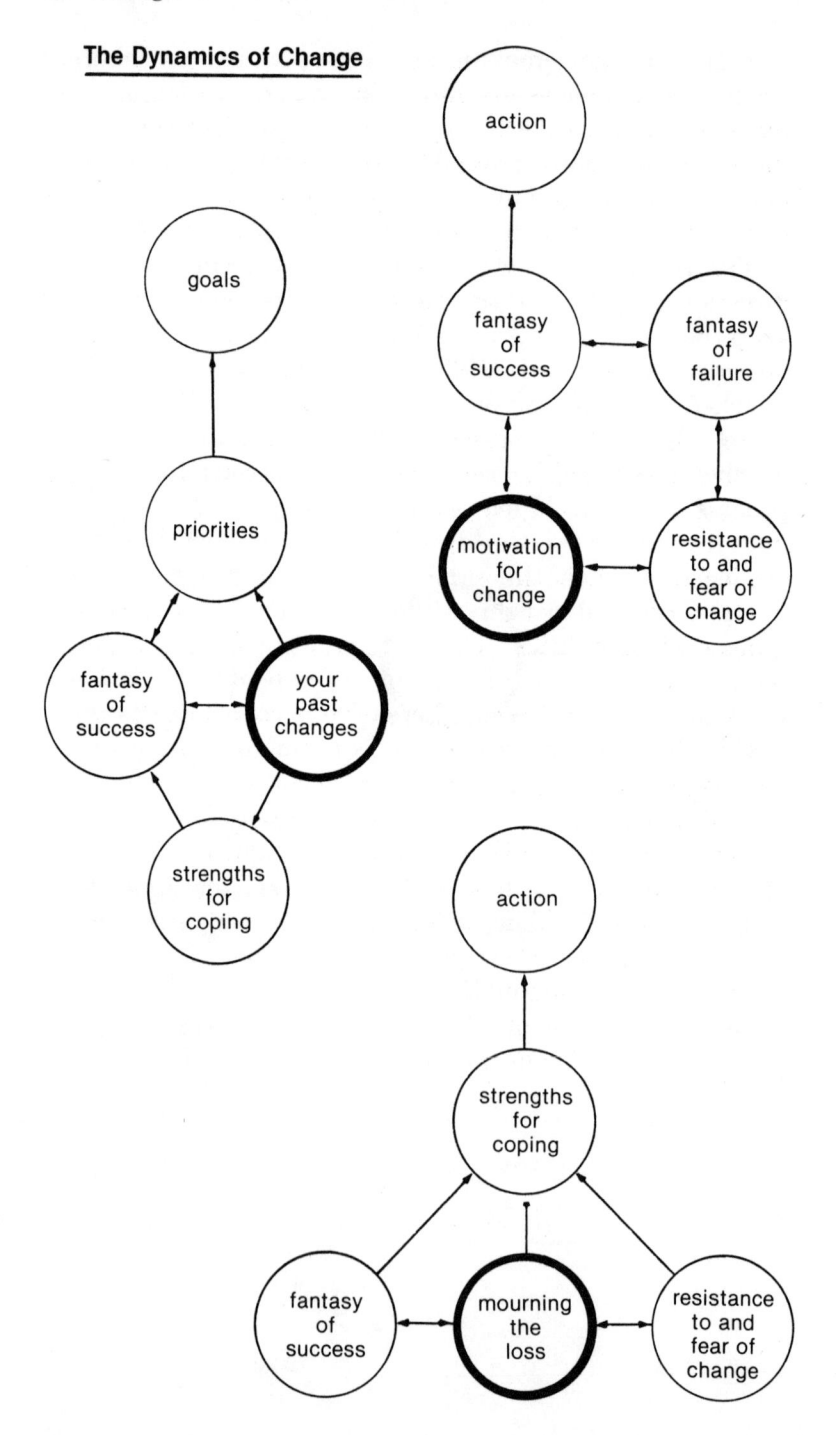

The Dynamics of Change

- goals
- priorities
- fantasy of success
- your past changes
- strengths for coping

- action
- fantasy of success
- fantasy of failure
- motivation for change
- resistance to and fear of change

- action
- strengths for coping
- fantasy of success
- mourning the loss
- resistance to and fear of change

The Journey Begins 33

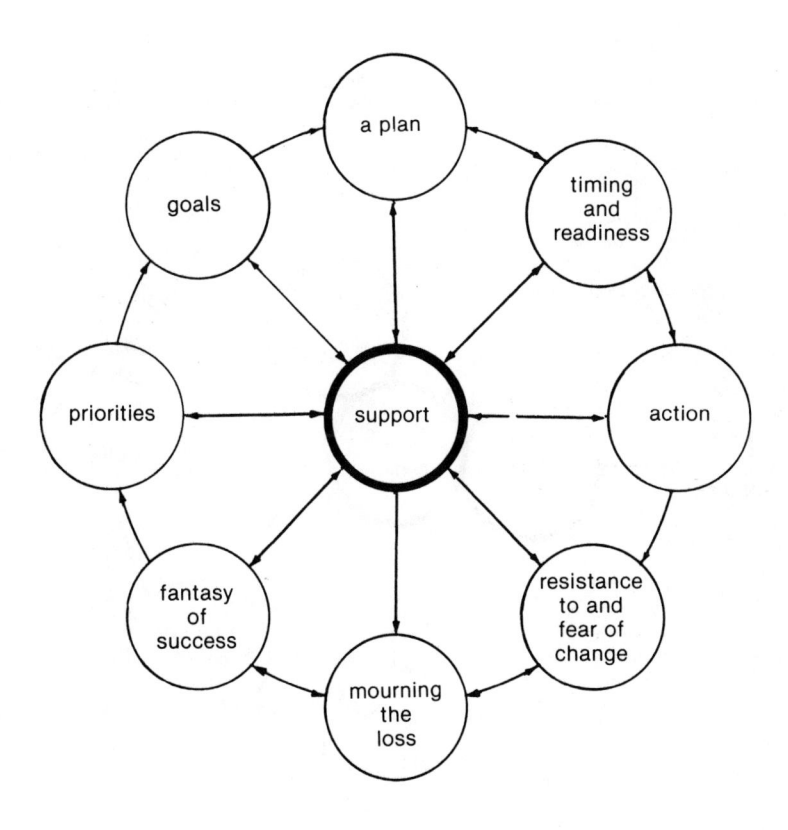

```
           a plan
    goals        timing
                 and
                 readiness

priorities    support    action

    fantasy       resistance
    of            to and
    success       fear of
                  change
           mourning
           the
           loss
```

34 Change

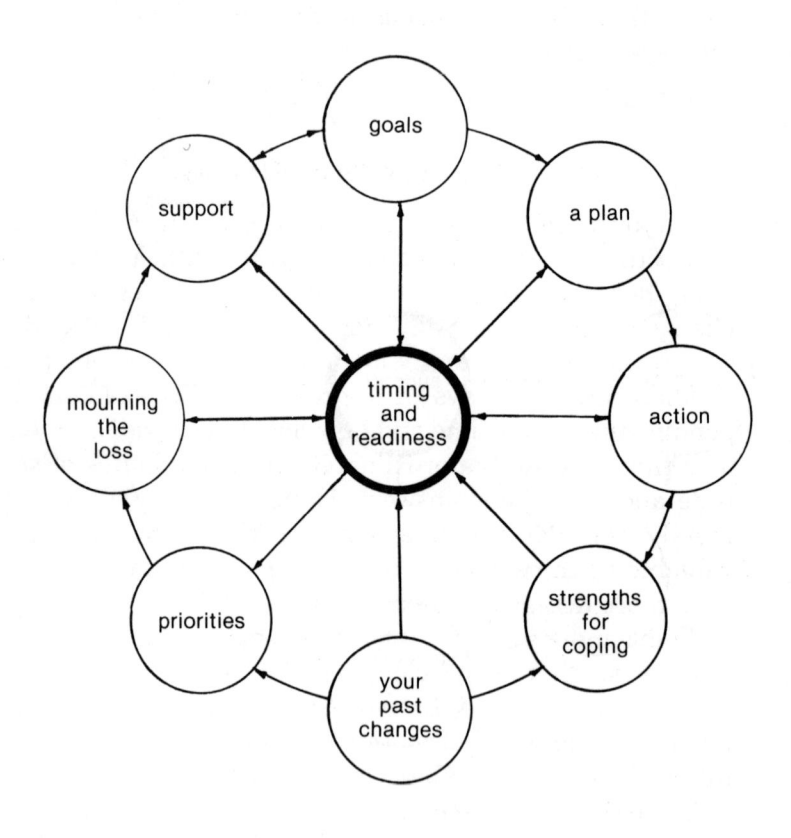

- goals
- a plan
- action
- strengths for coping
- your past changes
- priorities
- mourning the loss
- support

timing and readiness

Expanding Your Capacity

Now that you've gotten an overview of the change process, it's time to narrow your perspective and begin working more concentratedly. Although you already possess the necessary resources for change, you can certainly increase your capacity. I have designed several exercises toward this end with each one focusing on further developing one of the keys to change.

The first exercise pinpoints *Your Past Changes*.

Charting A Change History

The purpose of this exercise is to get you thinking and connecting to the past in a new way. It will help you to see your behavior patterns, to clarify your feelings and changemaking style. Following your own style instead of someone else's will greatly facilitate future changemaking.

There are two ways of approaching this exercise, depending upon your time and how deeply you wish to probe. The first is to find approximately twenty minutes of solitude and write your answers. However, you may wish to merely consider the questions, as it can be almost as valuable to think about your answers as to take the time for a more detailed self-examination.

Think more carefully about the many changes you've already weathered and compile a list. The purpose of this list is to help you see that you are an experienced changemaker, so you will feel more confident in approaching the future. I call this list Your Change History.

Make the list of the changes you've been through as long as you wish. Should you need ideas, here are several common life experiences which qualify as change:

- getting married
- becoming a parent or step-parent
- starting or quitting a job
- having an abortion
- learning to drive
- asking for a raise

- renting your first apartment
- being divorced or widowed
- buying a house
- having a nervous breakdown
- starting or leaving therapy
- losing fifty pounds
- going into or closing a business
- ending a close relationship
- becoming seriously ill
- retiring

The items on your list need not be placed in a chronological order. I'm sure that your memory follows associations of feelings rather than time sequences. Just write down whatever you think of, if it was important to you at the time.

As you review your life story, go back as far as you can remember. Take the list you have just compiled and be certain that you omitted no major event. This is *your* change history, so you are the only one who can judge the relevancy of each item. Select ten items from your list and enter them on the chart I have provided. Then ask the following questions for each change you made:

- Did I make this change with ease or difficulty?
- Was this change mostly a result of feeling or of thinking?
- Did I make this change largely on my own initiative, was I more influenced by others, or by circumstances largely out of my control? (The death of a loved one is out of your control.)
- What were my main reasons for making this change? What did I hope it would accomplish?
- How did I feel then about this change? How do I feel today?
- How long did it take me to make this change? This includes all prior activity related to the change as well as the length of time you needed to fully incorporate the change into your lifestyle.

Change History Chart

My Past Changes	Made with Ease or Difficulty?	A Result of Feeling or Thinking?	Made on my Own Initiative/ Others' Influences/ Circumstances	The Reasons	My Feelings Then/Now	The Time Involved	The Degree of Risk Involved

Think about how much risk-taking was involved in each of the changes on your list, and if risk-taking was difficult for you at the time.

See if you find any repeated patterns, ways of making changes that keep coming up. For instance, let's suppose that you rarely made your own decisions, that you typically abdicated responsibility for your life by letting others dictate what you should do. Just realize that not doing something or keeping silent is also a decision, involving your choice.

The way you were brought up influences how dependent or independent you feel as you risk change. Look at how you were treated as a child: as though you had the power and intelligence to make decisions for yourself, or considered helpless and in need of constant parental protection.

Later, when you are actively involved in making more changes, think about this exercise and your answers. Approach the future feeling connected to and using information from your past.

The second exercise identifies *Your Strengths*, and is a sequel to the previous exercise.

Your Reserve Bank

This is perhaps the most difficult exercise you will execute because, if you are like most of my clients, you are more accustomed to looking at your weaknesses than your strengths. So take your time. You'll probably enjoy doing this exercise with a close friend. Each of you can provide for the other the feedback and objectivity that you can't as easily give to yourselves.

Use the changes you listed in the previous exercise, Charting A Change History. Answer the following question in terms of each change:

• What strengths helped me to cope as I made this change—what characteristics did I either have or develop to assist me?

You have a considerable reserve bank of strengths. Don't

minimize the importance of your using them. Here are several strengths my clients discovered they possessed.

- know when I need help, able to ask for it
- listen to others' suggestions
- in touch with my feelings, communicate them clearly
- make a decision and take the consequences
- able to compromise
- able to help someone even when I feel anxious
- make and keep friends
- take risks
- able to cope with uncertainty
- survived a negative environment
- able to take responsibility
- flexible
- tenacious
- independent

Fill in the following chart for *each* of the changes you mentioned in Charting A Change History.

Past Changes I Made	Strengths Which Helped Me To Cope
	1.
	2.
	3.
	4.
	5.

Do you remember the diagrams shown earlier in this chapter? So far, we covered this much territory:

```
        your
        past
      changes
         ↓
   strengths
      for
    coping
```

Now let's add one more concept.

```
   fantasy ←→  your
     of         past
  success     changes
       ↖      ↙
        strengths
           for
         coping
```

The future will seem like less of a void when you complete the last two exercises, Charting A Change History and Your Reserve Bank. Understanding what you've accomplished in the past and knowing your strengths allow you to face whatever is ahead more optimistically.

So let's leave the past and move forward again in time. You're going to use the often untapped resources of your right brain, the seat of the artistic and intuitive. In its magic is the source of your power to effect change.

Fantasy is quite powerful, not an irrelevant or unrealistic plaything relegated only to childhood or psychologically warped minds. Consider the notion that fantasizing fully utilizes your creativity, imagination and inspiration. Think of fantasizing as a tangible tool for actualizing your dreams. In a highly technological society, we may have lost or hidden our spiritual side. We're entirely too sensible, logical and grounded in reality.

You can recapture the beauty of childhood innocence. Unpin your butterfly wings. Be a visionary. Indulge in flights of fancy, build castles in the air, follow the rainbow, pretend. Don't let any concern about practicality curb your imagination. Living without art is like being a robot with no heart. Rediscover your spiritual self.

The next exercise will help you to do this, through developing *Your Fantasy Of Success.*

Skyhooks

Dream about the kind of life you'd really like. Let your dreams give you the skyhooks you need for reaching to the moon. Create a fantasy of success for tomorrow.

The value of this exercise is that by visualizing success, you can make it happen. It's not really magic—it's the power of positive thinking. Talk is cheap, action is vital, but talking about change can make it more of a reality. You'll also speed up the changemaking process by envisioning and then sharing your dreams.

Paint a picture, write a story or tape a statement about your fantasy life. Then verbalize this daydream, using the present tense, as though you have projected yourself into the future in a time machine. Be there *now*. Give it a time reference: date your fantasy a week from today or sometime within the next six months. Be specific. Add color and texture, make it three-dimensional by describing what you're doing and where, with whom (if you are not alone) and why. What are your feelings? How do you spend most of your time? Make it the most marvelously easy way of life without worrying about how you got here. Don't worry about what seems feasible, sensible or practical. Have fun with designing your world—exactly as you want it, with no restrictions. Let your imagination run wild.

Let's see what information can be obtained from someone's fantasy of success:

One of my clients is a teacher who, although not ready to leave her job, is certainly thinking about it. Because Elsie has never before had the opportunity to consider her own needs, she really has no idea of what she'd like to do. Elsie drew herself lounging at the water's edge on a sunny beach, enjoying the fresh sea breezes and leisurely collecting seashells. When I asked her to elaborate, she told me that she was living in a small cottage in a fairly sparsely populated area. Everyone had a similar outlook and therefore got on well together. Elsie was happy and had no major worries.

Further discussion clarified and focused what Elsie was saying through her fantasy. Because she had recently been through a lot, what Elsie especially craved was peace, quiet, pleasure and not feeling pushed. Both physically and emotionally, the space she described was a very different one than she was now in. Elsie cut out all the frills, not needing a big house or a great number of people—yet she still had enough intimacy and a lifestyle which afforded great satisfaction.

It isn't really a question of whether or not Elsie intends to go off to a tropical place. She can decide this later. Elsie found that this exercise helped her to do what she had previously been unable to do: identify what she wanted. Even what she omitted was important: extraordinary wealth, specific work, being taken care of by someone else, dealing with practical matters. Her fantasy affirms Elsie's need for a simpler existence, for remembering what is really important, what life is all about.

What is your fantasy? Add one more facet: what *you* did to get to this place.

Remember to fill in as many details as possible and to stay in the present tense as though the experience is real *now*. What are the feelings, issues and values your fantasy represents? Give it a more holistic interpretation, reading the content poetically, rather than literally. What is the world you just designed telling you about yourself and your future direction?

As you delve more deeply into changemaking, review this exercise. See what new dreams come up.

(Your Fantasy of Failure will be covered in Chapter 3.)

So far you've covered three of the Keys To Change. Now we're going to explore the next one, *Your Priorities*.

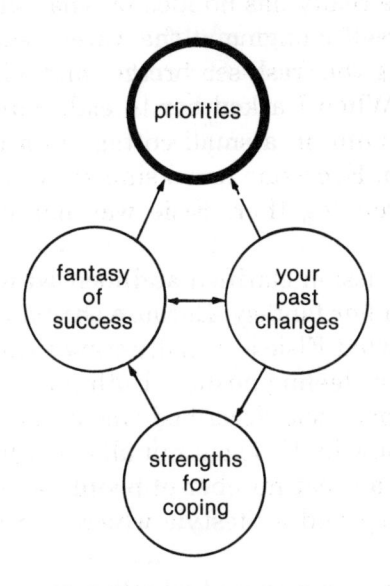

```
                    priorities
                   ↗    ↑    ↖
          fantasy          your
            of     ←→      past
          success         changes
                   ↖    ↑    ↗
                   strengths
                      for
                    coping
```

From the darker corners of your mind, you've plucked gossamer threads, golden dreams to lighten all your tomorrows. Dreams are merely vehicles transporting you to the secret recesses of your soul—messages telling you what you really care about, what your priorities are.

In a world that is sometimes chaotic or superficial, I know how hard it is to live by your priorities. Just attempting this is what makes my own life that much more meaningful.

When a ceramicist works at the wheel to center a pot, she looks for that delicate balance between inner and outer pressure in order to prevent the piece from collapsing. To me, there can be a similar balance achieved in a person's lifestyle: a congruity between what you feel and think and value and the way you choose to live. Such congruence gives you a sense of integrity. Its lack leads to your feeling unhappy, disillusioned, purposeless or that something is missing. I believe that in the long run, if you are patient, living with this integrity will result in enduring success.

Let's begin with identifying your building blocks, the ingredients necessary for a happier life. If you're somewhat uncertain as to exactly what your priorities are, ask yourself:

- What is missing from my life?
- What is really important to me? Why?

Answer in only a few words, using nouns. Here is a sample list of priorities. Add others which you feel are equally important:

____financial stability	____communication
____inner peace	____contact with people
____health	____popularity
____security	____continuity
____status	____feedback
____power	____being needed
____recognition	____intimacy
____beauty	____pleasure
____nature	____privacy
____solitude	____a sense of belonging
____creativity	____mobility
____variety	____challenge
____freedom, autonomy	____interdependence, mutuality
____love	____influence
____sensuality	____sexuality
____family ties	____a sense of achievement
____	____
____	____
____	____
____	____

Which priorities are uppermost for you? Which ones can you pretty much do without? To clarify this, ask yourself:

- What would I be willing to give up to get what I want? Would I do this just for myself or only for someone else?
- For which priorities do I have such a strong need—or

a sense of conviction—that I would stand up and "fight" to achieve them if necessary?

- Am I really a fighter, or do I prefer to take a less active role?

Next, rank your priorities according to the value you place upon each, giving the most important priority the highest number. This is not easy to decide! The surest way of knowing is through your gut level feelings, not with your head.

When I first resigned a relatively lucrative position in order to freelance, I was certain that I was willing to forego certain priorities in order to have others. The ones I temporarily gave up were: security, continuity, a sense of belonging, financial stability, a certain degree of status (although I expected to achieve more). What I wanted was solitude, a wider impact, autonomy, challenge, variety, mobility, more responsibility, and creativity. When these were attained, I looked forward to setting new priorities. Life consists of such constant renewal. You're never going to be completely settled, unless you stop growing and dreaming.

Your priorities serve mainly as guideposts. Be patient. Don't expect immediate gratification. Stating that something is of importance to you today makes it more likely to be a significant part of your life in the future.

When setting priorities there are several steps to follow.

- Ask yourself questions about what you need, want and expect from life.
- Check whether your current lifestyle is congruent with who you are.
- Be honest with yourself. Know who you are, what you feel and what is missing from your life.
- Follow your own standards, not what you think you *should* feel or want, or what someone else wants.
- Be selfish. It's the only way you'll be true to yourself!
- Write down your priorities.
- Ask whether these priorities feel "right" and will im-

prove the quality of your work, relationships and life, and whether they will make you happier.
• Know specifically why these priorities are meaningful to you.
• Keep your priorities uppermost in mind every day.
• Know when they have become a stable part of your life so you don't continue the quest needlessly.
• Reevaluate and reset your priorities when they no longer seem important or when you've incorporated them into your daily life.

Priorities are only one step in a sequence. The next step is setting easily attainable goals based on them.

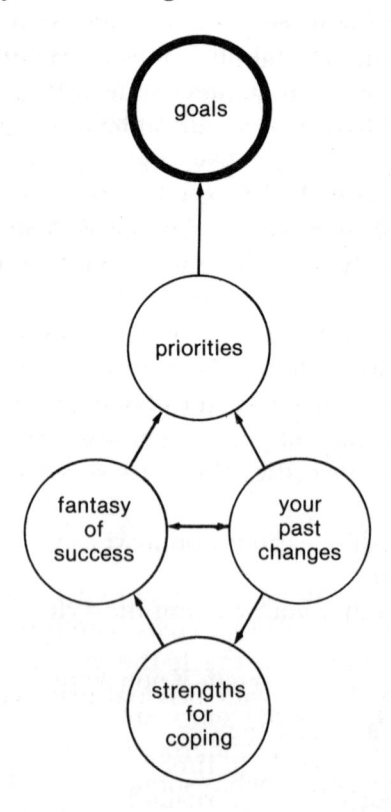

```
                    goals
                      ↑
                      |
                  priorities
                  ↗       ↖
           fantasy         your
             of            past
           success ←→    changes
                  ↖       ↗
                 strengths
                    for
                  coping
```

If the word "goal" is too vague or overwhelming, substitute the question: What do I hope to accomplish?
To double check that it is indeed a goal based upon one

or more of your priorities, ask: Why do I want this? What will I gain if I do reach this goal?

If your answers do not include a top priority, change the goal!

Some people put the cart before the horse by setting goals before they've looked at their priorities. A case in point is Joanie, who for over fifteen years was late to work. Joanie's goal was to get to work on time, but because there were no reprisals, nothing she tried made any difference. She felt frustrated and stymied.

When a goal hasn't been reached for so long, my first suspicion is that the goal is inappropriate. Two possible reasons are that it is not based upon one of your priorities, or that the goal has not been selected with enough understanding or self-examination. With this premise in mind, Joanie and I worked on restating her goal. Eventually Joanie suggested a priority that promptly produced a resolution of the problem. She realized that what she had always wanted was not to get to work on time, but to be able to start her day without feeling so rushed. She wanted time to herself which she could spend in a more relaxed manner. Joanie's priority was time to herself. Now she gets up an hour earlier every day and watches television quietly. This newfound space gives her such a feeling of calmness that Joanie is happy. Another benefit is that she also is on time!

The next exercise will help you set *Your Goals*.

Goal-Digging

Goal-Digging requires that you take a shovel and persist until you hit rock bottom. When searching for your goals, keep asking "Why?" to reach the goal beneath the goal, until all that is left is your original priority. For example, here is Joanie's Goal-Digging:

Goal. To get to work on time.
Why ? Because I feel so rushed.
Goal. To feel less rushed.
Why do you want to feel less rushed? Because I never seem to have enough time for myself.

Is this important? Yes, my priority is to have more time for myself, without feeling rushed.

New goal. To find more time for myself without pressure.

Check your motivation carefully. If you're thinking of ending a relationship, decide if that's what you really want or whether you'd rather improve it if you could. Is your priority independence or improved communication?

Be sure your goal is small enough to provide a first step. For example, having the goal "to get married" is too general. Start with more specific objectives, such as: to explore organized social events, to meet more eligible men (or women), to become more involved in activities that might extend your friendships, and to develop more intimacy in your current friendships.

When formulating goals, ask yourself these questions:

- In whose voice is this goal? Am I stating what *I* want or what I think I should be doing? Is it important to *me*?
- Upon what priorities is it based?
- Am I being positive rather than negative—stating what I do *want* to do, rather than what I don't want to do?
- Am I loving in the way I have stated my goals, giving myself options, room to breathe?

Go back to your priority list and select the three top priorities. Next set goals to help you make these priorities really a part of your life. These suggestions will simplify the process.

1. Since goals imply action, use phrases with verbs to describe them. Examples are: ask, see, decide, go, write, call, find, get, list, explore, or complete.

2. Be sure that the goal you choose is something over which you have control. Otherwise you'll be dooming yourself to failure. For example, you can ask for a raise, but really do not have the power to decide that you will get one. Therefore the goal properly stated might be: to *ask* for a raise, rather than to *get* a raise.

3. A goal must be specific rather than general. If your goal is to increase your income, decide by what exact amount. Then modify your goal: to increase my income by $1,000 (or $10,000).

4. Put your goals into a time-slot. You may decide to separate them into short and long range goals. Be sure that your short range goals can be accomplished in days and weeks, not months and years!

5. Do not make your goals too broad in scope or they will be impossible to attain. Make them manageable.

6. Be sure that these goals are based upon your own priorities, and that you really know why you've set them.

7. Keep them current. Reevaluate and reset whenever it seems necessary so that they are up to date.

8. Simplify and clarify your wording so that your goals are stated as briefly as possible.

9. Articulate your goals in as many ways as you can. Write them, talk about them, try them on for size. Make your goals a focus at some point every day. Do not get sidetracked.

10. Make a commitment to reaching your goals, even though you may decide to alter them later.

Piecework

So far, you have gotten an overview of the change process, been introduced to the Twelve Keys To Change and worked on several of them in depth. Throughout the book, we will build on what you've already accomplished, through additional material and different exercises.

You may have noticed that some keys to change required more of your attention than others, as a result of your prior experiences and training. To equalize them, first identify which Keys To Change are your strongest. Put a check next to them on the chart which follows. Also check the ones of which you feel the least sure.

As you continue, recognize where you still have the greatest difficulty and spend time repeating the exercises that apply. Bit by bit, piece by piece, you'll gradually strengthen any weak spots and reach a more balanced synthesis.

Keys To Change	Where I'm Strongest	Where I Most Need To Work
1. Past Changes	_____	_____
2. My Strengths	_____	_____
3. Fantasy of Success and Failure	_____	_____
4. Priorities	_____	_____
5. Goals	_____	_____
6. Motivation for Change	_____	_____
7. Fear and Resistance	_____	_____
8. Mourning	_____	_____
9. Support	_____	_____
10. Timing and Readiness	_____	_____
11. A Plan	_____	_____
12 Action	_____	_____

Congratulate yourself. You've successfully faced the void, chosen a destination and are well on your journey. How quickly you proceed now depends upon which is stronger: your motivation or your resistance. Until you gather up enough energy to shift the balance, you'll remain in the same place. So now your next step is to examine your ambivalence for change.

Part Two: Interference

Chapter 3: The Pull of the Status Quo

Cross-Currents Of Ambivalence

Some people let nothing stand in their way when they want something. Others resign themselves to making the best of a situation, even though they'd prefer things to be different. However, let's not assume that people who take the initiative are more motivated and more confident than those who wait. In fact, they may feel just as hesitant. The important difference is that they have learned how to act in spite of their fear.

You probably harbor many misconceptions about how motivated you're supposed to feel before taking a major step. Once you've taken a deep breath and plotted your course, do you expect to proceed serenely, with no setbacks or deviation?

Please don't be so hard on yourself. With such unrealistic expectations, any slight waning of your enthusiasm will make you anxious, convinced that there must be something terribly wrong with you. If you've been trying to be the picture of perfection, remember that you're only human. Don't wait for one hundred percent motivation before you take another step, because you'll be waiting forever! There will always be fears, obstacles and setbacks that provoke grave doubts about your initial decision. You'll never feel quite motivated enough to be completely worry-free. In fact, you'll experience not only a forward thrust toward a particular change, but also a strong counter-pull in the opposite direction, toward the status quo. This internal tug-of-war is merely your healthy ambivalence:

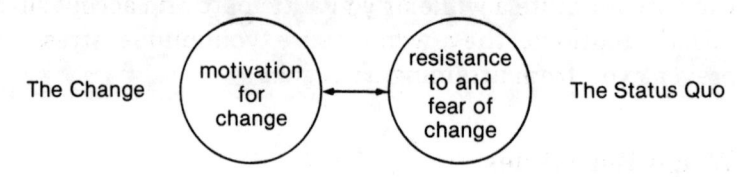

The Change (motivation for change) ←→ (resistance to and fear of change) The Status Quo

Ambivalence

Ambivalence is normal.

It's natural to feel excited about having a baby and still wonder whether you're capable of taking on this added responsibility. When looking forward to the challenge of a second career, you may worry that no one will hire you. In the early stages of making a change, many people experience such swings of emotion:

Ephraim was looking for a new job, but lost the resume he was about to mail to a prospective employer—twice. That's when Ephraim realized he felt ambivalent.

When her unemployment insurance was about to end, Teresa emphatically told me, "Now I'll *have* to find a job," but often stayed at home to sleep. Nevertheless, Teresa projected enough confidence to be offered three different jobs. After deliberating, she chose a high salaried executive position.

Jodie is a talented and well-known freelance photographer who'd much rather avoid looking for work than face possible rejection.

Harry finally got a divorce after procrastinating for several months.

Mary kept declaring, "I'll get a doctorate when I am truly motivated," until she realized that it wasn't such a practical goal. Instead, after a second master's degree, Mary changed her profession. Now she is a management consultant for a major corporation at a much higher salary.

Prepare yourself for some degree of hesitation, insecurity or ambivalence when you're making a change. You may vacillate for quite a while. If you anticipate and accept such mixed emotions, they won't cause you undue stress or prevent you from attaining each goal.

Weigh Both Sides

It is unwise to go forging ahead just because you made a commitment. Rather than being compulsive about it, act from an awareness of your true feelings. Ask yourself:
- Do I sincerely wish this change?
- Or does the status quo suit me better?

Carefully probe your thoughts and emotions by fantasizing, drawing, writing or discussing them with a friend. Fantasy is an excellent tool. It provides a rapid nonverbal experience packed with valuable information you might otherwise overlook.

There are two fantasies of importance here: your fantasy of success and a fantasy of failure.

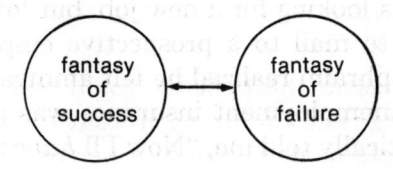

fantasy of success ↔ fantasy of failure

Your Fantasies

Each has a distinct function. Your motivation and your fantasy of success push you toward action. Your fear of change and fantasy of failure keep you in the status quo.

Let's look at the positive side first.

You've already explored your fantasy of success. What did you visualize? (If necessary, refresh your memory by reviewing Skyhooks, in Chapter 2.)

Now consider your motivation. What are your main reasons for wanting to go ahead? Present a strong case of the "pro" position by including the priorities on which such

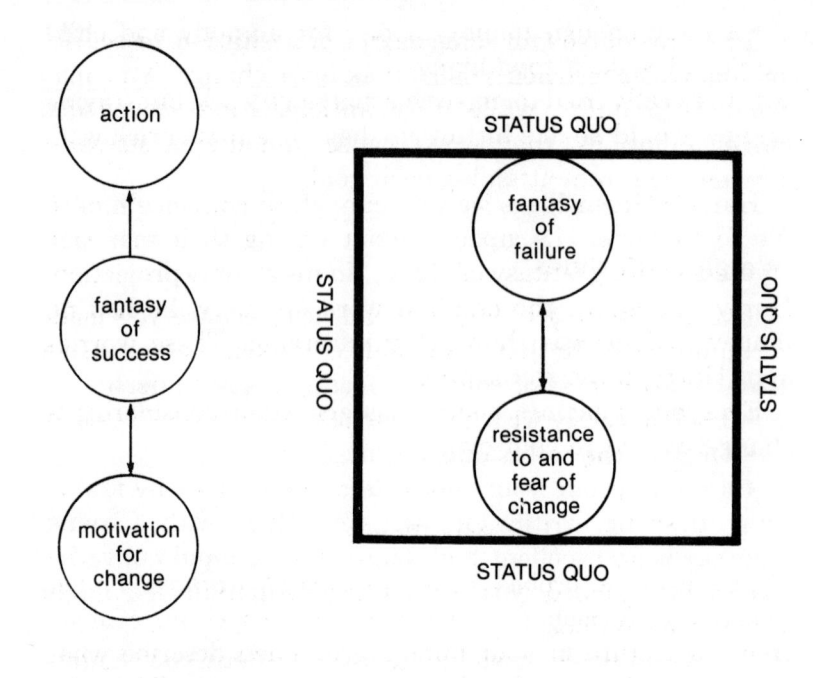

```
        action                    STATUS QUO

                              ┌─────────────────┐
                              │    fantasy      │
                              │      of         │
                              │    failure      │
       fantasy          STATUS │       ↕         │ STATUS
         of              QUO   │                 │  QUO
       success                 │   resistance    │
                              │    to and       │
                              │   fear of       │
                              │    change       │
      motivation              └─────────────────┘
         for
        change                     STATUS QUO
```

The Positive Side   **The Hesitant Side**

a decision is based, the benefits you'll gain through this particular change and the strengths that will help you cope. Make short statements in the first person. They are your Green Flags, clear signals to proceed.

These were Harry's Green Flags, when he contemplated getting a divorce after fifteen years of marriage:

Green Flags

- I'll be able to do what I want when I want.
- I'd like a more honest relationship than this one.
- I don't wish to live with someone I no longer love or respect.
- The children will be better off if we separate.
- I'm tired of being taken for granted.
- I'll be happier living alone than I am now.
- I want my freedom and I am willing to take a risk.

- I have enough money to pay for alimony and child support. I make a good living.
- I've really tried to make this marriage work, but staying on now would be like hitting my head against a brick wall.

Harry's Green Flags weren't enough to convince him to file for divorce. His anxiety about ending their marriage created a strong fantasy of failure. In his gloomy projection, Harry was alone, the children were unhappy, he had no money and he was thoroughly miserable. These worries kept Harry in the status quo.

Everyone imagines such disasters when considering a change. What are your own?

Dark Clouds

This exercise probes *Your Fantasy Of Failure*. To get closer to your deeper feelings about a prospective change, create a picture in your mind's eye. Then describe what you see by writing, drawing or taping (as you did in the exercise Skyhooks).

First visualize yourself making a specific change. Then imagine the most terrible thing that could happen to you as a result. Complete the scene with these details:

- your location: place, surroundings, time of day
- the person(s) you are with (unless you are alone)
- what you are doing
- how you are feeling
- exactly how you coped with all that transpired
- what *you* did or didn't do that put you in this place

Then look at your finished work.

To give the scene a present reality, speak about it as though it were happening *now*. Interpret your fantasy poetically, as you did your fantasy of success. Try not to take it too literally.

What insights does your fantasy inspire?

To be sure that your dark clouds are followed by a rainbow, add The Clincher.

The Clincher. Each time you fantasize failure, say out loud:

"It's all right for me to fail at this. I am a worthwhile person even if I fail."

Suddenly what you do or don't do becomes less important. Life is no longer a struggle against impossible odds. The pressure is off. You're relaxed and comfortable.

No one performs as well under the heavy burden of "I can't fail!" Giving yourself permission to fail at something makes it much more likely that you will succeed.

Your fantasy of failure is fed by a long list of fears about taking this step. To clarify them, think about the following:

- Why haven't I attempted this before?
- What frightens me the most? Why?
- What risks are involved?

Whenever you feel incapable of achieving something or believe that if you do reach your goal, nothing will work out, such worries keep you immobile. These doubts are your Red Flags, raised to prevent you from changing your life. Where Dark Clouds used images to clarify your feelings, Red Flags expresses them verbally.

Here are Harry's Red Flags about being divorced:

Red Flags

- It's a jungle out there. I know what to expect here, so I'd better stay.
- There's no one around as smart/attractive/loving as she.
- It's too risky/costly/much trouble to get a divorce.
- I'm such a failure. I'm grateful that she puts up with me. No one else would.
- Our children couldn't cope with a divorce.
- She needs me, and so do they.
- This is what all marriages are like. I can't expect anything better than this.
- No one else will find me attractive. I'll be alone forever if I leave.

- I'm unable to make a decision. I might make the wrong one.
- I couldn't possibly survive economically. Divorce is a drain.
- I'm anxious about what my friends and relatives will think of me if I get a divorce. It would also ruin me professionally.

What are your own Red Flags about the change you're considering?

Externalizing your deepest feelings further clarifies them. However, if seeing how conflicted you really feel makes you think you're still in square one, relax.

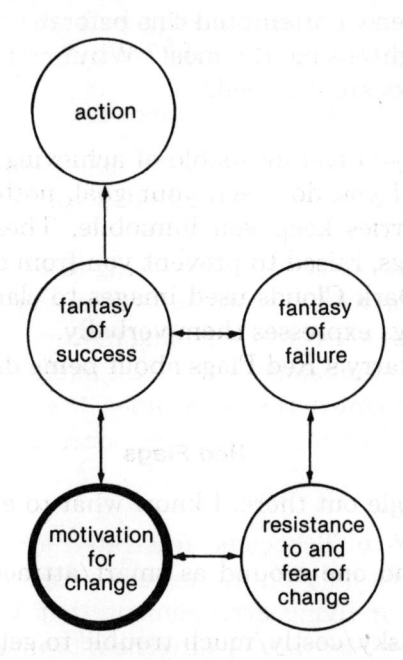

```
              action
                ↑
    fantasy         fantasy
      of    ←─────    of
    success         failure
       ↑               ↑
    motivation  ←   resistance
       for           to and
     change          fear of
                     change
```

You Can Proceed In Spite of Ambivalence

You can take action in spite of your ambivalence through these ten simple steps.

1. Think of a change you are considering. Fantasize the change successfully achieved.
2. Look at all the reasons that push you in this direction.
3. Fantasize your own failures.

4. Then state your darkest fears.
5. Expect, accept this ambivalence.
6. Trust that you'll eventually find a better balance between your motivation and reluctance. Give yourself the time to get centered.
7. When you do feel more centered, get your feet wet by taking a tiny step in the direction of the change.
8. Experience whatever feeling arise.
9. Repeat the process as many times as necessary, and check which is strongest and most persistent: your motivation or resistance to the change.
10. Then decide whether or not you are ready to make this change.

You've already accomplished steps 1 to 5. The following exercise will guide you along the remaining five steps.

Embracing Opposites

This exercise eases any anxiety about constant vacillation between extremes and facilitates your reaching a balance.

Exaggerate your tendency to swing to opposite poles by fully embracing each position as it comes up.

For example, when you're feeling most complacent about your present circumstances and least likely to make a shift, don't try. Remember the good times, the joyful moments, the small satisfactions you've experienced. Give in to your pleasure.

Let time pass.

Eventually, you'll become frustrated again about your situation. Focus only on the negative aspects of the relationship, job or living arrangement that you wish were different. Allow any rage or bitterness to mount.

You needn't worry about getting stuck in either position, because of the Pendulum Principle.

The Pendulum Principle. Your motion in changemaking is very much that of a pendulum—broad swings from one side to the other in smaller and smaller arcs. Gradually, the pendulum will come to rest in the middle. Allowing yourself the experience of both extremes reinforces this middle ground.

These questions serve to focus your anxiety and gently ease you closer to taking a few small steps in the direction you've chosen. Think about your answers this week.

1. How much responsibility for your life are you willing to assume?
2. How much are you influenced by what others think?
3. What usually provokes your decisions?
4. Whose needs are most important to you? Why?
5. When was the last time that you failed at something?
6. When was the last time you succeeded?
7. With which are you more comfortable: failure or success?
8. Are you a fighter? For what (or whom) have you fought? What were the results?
9. What guarantees would you need in order to proceed?
10. What three simple and failproof steps could you take this week toward your goal?

The best way to make a change is from a centered position. People who are centered have the following qualities. They:
- feel relaxed, yet ready to move
- confront their feelings
- act by their own standards, not other people's
- accept ambivalence
- give themselves the time to experience and work through any doubts
- desire a change more than they fear it
- flow with opposition instead of fighting against it
- bounce quickly back from defeats and rejection
- take risks and accept the consequences of their actions

How many of these characteristics do you already possess?

Which ones do you need to develop over the next weeks?

Tuning In

The purpose of this exercise is to help you monitor your feelings and determine which is stronger—your motivation or resistance. Either use a tape recorder to record your comments, work with someone, or tune in to yourself in the next few days as you speak about this change to your friends.

First state what the change is. For instance, you might say, "I'm planning to go back to school for my bachelor's degree." Then tell why you're considering doing this, what you hope to gain and what you are afraid will happen if you proceed. Go into as much detail as you can. Suspend judgment. Merely report what you feel at this moment as you speak.

If you are taping, play back your conversation. If you are with a friend, ask him to give you feedback on what he saw and heard.

Be receptive to your true feelings. Hear beneath the words. Take nothing at face value. Use your intuition, not your intellect. Trust your ability to sense both stated and unstated emotions.

What feelings does your tone of voice communicate?

Listen not only with your ears, but also with your body. Allow it to tell you what you were then and are now experiencing.

How did your body react during the time you spoke? Where was there tension?

A sensitive partner will experience your feelings kinesthetically by mirroring them with his body. For example, he may feel your tightness in his throat, butterflies or shortness of breath.

What nonverbal behavior did he observe?

Did you clench your fists, shift in your chair, hold your breath, smile or frown as you spoke?

What kinds of feelings does duplicating such gestures now evoke?

Overall, on which side of the scale was the balance weighted? Was your motivation for change or your resistance stronger?

Ambivalence does not last forever. Before each shift where some degree of risk is involved, I experience feelings of ambivalence. I might be weighing a decision to move to a new apartment, sign a book contract, start an affair or turn down a lecturing engagement. If the issue is important to me, I spend time with friends whose opinions I trust. Our discussions help me to clarify the benefits and drawbacks and make a decision that feels comfortable.

What gets me through these periods is the ability to live comfortably with conflicting feelings. I am tolerant because I have a perspective on ambivalence from prior experience. I know that doubts will vanish and in their place will come a sense of conviction—because that's what has always happened.

Negativity is necessary. Fear is not an enemy. When you can accept your resistance to and fear of change, it won't prevent you from acting.

Chapter 4: Understanding Resistance to Change

Why You May Still Resist Change

In spite of a strong motivation, are you still reluctant to take action?

We cling to the status quo when changing makes us uneasy. There are several factors which might cause you to have a resistant attitude:

- Your social conditioning acts as a deterrent.
- A lack of expertise makes you feel inadequate.
- Unclear priorities or a focus on the wrong issues result in confusion.
- Inappropriate timing for initiating action makes you feel unready.
- You're ashamed of feeling afraid, believing that fear is a negative emotion to be avoided at all costs.

We will explore each of these factors more carefully, so you can get a broader perspective of your own resistance.

Negative Social Conditioning

Cindy's father was severely critical of her appearance, speech and behavior. In school, the other children made Cindy the scapegoat because of her obvious shyness. As she grew up, Cindy became a fearful person who doubted her ability to cope with any unfamiliar situation.

Hugh finds it difficult to make changes. He would like to

be more assertive and to take greater risks but lacks the courage to break habitual patterns. Hugh works in a Fortune 500 firm where acceptable attire and roles are unstated but clearly understood. In Hugh's executive position he is expected to determine policy for two departments, yet the company's very conservative attitude sorely limits his options.

When Yvette first came to my support group, she wouldn't take a step without first receiving everyone's tacit approval. This dependent attitude prevented Yvette from enjoying her own decisions. With the group's encouragement, Yvette began to make more decisions by herself and stopped worrying about what anyone else thought.

One's family background, work and social environment either promotes or discourages change. Cindy's upbringing certainly did nothing to foster her self-assurance. It is no wonder then that she faces any prospective change with considerably less confidence and greater fear than most other people. In Hugh's case there is a carryover into his private life from a work environment where risk-taking is rare. Since Yvette's friends did not encourage her growth, she used the support group as a substitute social environment. This helped Yvette to feel more confident. In all three examples, social conditioning influenced the individual to maintain the status quo.

Look at your own situation. If you usually feel comfortable with change, assume that your social conditioning has been supportive of your growth. If, on the other hand, change makes you uneasy, look at the reasons behind your attitude.

Most people are programmed against change by their family, friends, employers, neighbors and the society-at-large. The pressure to conform is very strong. We're not supposed to rock the boat or make waves. Neither the self-confrontation and solitude needed for preliminary self-assessment, nor the individuality and creativity change requires are reinforced by commonly accepted social values. Instead, we're encouraged to keep a stiff upper lip, deny that there is anything wrong with our lifestyle or be so busy that we cannot even stop to think.

A Lack of Expertise

June and Billy travelled to Chile to adopt a child and then decided to settle there. This meant that they had to find a source of income, learn a new language and customs and leave many friends behind. Neither June nor Billy had previously made a comparable move. Yet together they made up in enthusiasm and resourcefulness whatever they lacked in experience. The couple opened up a food store, quickly established new friendships and is now managing nicely.

The men and women in my career-change seminars who have worked for over twenty-years in one field are neophytes when it comes to job-hunting strategies. As a result, they don't know where to start, how to assess their interests and abilities, research possible fields, market themselves or plan a job campaign. Each participant assumes that everyone else has greater skills to offer prospective employers. Fear and anxiety about the change are common. Yet I know of countless people, including myself, who made a career change successfully—in midlife.

Countless new divorcees are faced with problems for which they feel completely unprepared. After being married for years, now there is the added responsibility of raising a child alone, without the emotional or practical assistance of a mate. The last time many of them went on a date was at least twenty years ago. Current mores are confusing. They are not sure what is expected of them, or how to behave. Gradually, with practice, they feel more adept socially, start to relax and have fun. A few may even develop greater intimacy than they had within their marriage.

Do you lack experience for the change you are considering?

Although you probably think you're supposed to feel very competent, it's perfectly all right to admit that you don't. There is a subtle pressure to avoid saying, even to yourself, "I don't know." But such high standards are impractical and unreasonable. No one is an expert in everything. It is natural to feel anxious or fearful when you attempt something for the very first time. Involvement in an unfamiliar area places you in a rank beginner status. Lacking experience and know-how, you'll undoubtedly falter and make mistakes.

The more times you have gone through an experience, the greater your confidence will be when you face it again. Through the trial-and-error of past efforts, you have gathered considerable information and now know better what to expect, how to proceed and where to get assistance.

Try not to dwell in anger or frustration because of temporary ignorance. Be patient with yourself. If you lack experience, give yourself the time to acquire it. If you lack certain skills, try to figure out which ones you need to work on. (For instance, if you are having difficulty setting goals, refer back to your Preliminary Goal List and Goal-Digging exercise.) Perhaps it's planning that is bothering you. Planning involves goal-setting, organizing a procedure to follow, choosing between alternatives, getting information, assistance or additional resources.

Which one of these skills is your strongest?

Where do you need more practice?

Unclear Priorities

Everyone excitedly talked about impending vacation plans to Randy, who ignored their comments and kept silent. When friends insisted, "You've been working so hard and surely need a vacation. How are you going to spend it?" she didn't know how to answer. Randy felt pressured, but had no idea of where to go. For weeks, every time she considered a possible option, Randy experienced distress.

Ethan was considering buying a dog because he likes animals and thought that owning a dog would be rewarding. He shopped for months without finding an animal that pleased him. Ethan didn't know what was wrong or why this decision was so difficult.

Both Randy and Ethan put off making a minor decision because it caused them anxiety. Yet the longer each postponed it, the more uncomfortable he or she became. Later,

Randy and Ethan realized that they were procrastinating because neither of them wanted the change. Randy was busy with many interesting projects and had no interest in or need for a vacation. Ethan worried about the daily walks, grooming, training and attention a dog would require. Upon further thought, Ethan decided against this extra responsibility even though it meant forgoing the obvious pleasure a pet would bring.

When you are considering a change, make certain that it is based upon a priority of yours. Try not to be overly influenced as Randy was by others' opinions or activities. Look at all the issues involved. Ask yourself:

- Would this change require a different focus or direction than I have now?
- Would it mean added responsibilities?
- Is it based on *my* priorities rather than on someone else's?
- Is this change one that *really* want?

You can waste a great deal of energy fretting about something that is not really a priority.

Inappropriate Timing

Within six months after his wife's death, Sheldon closed the dry goods business that they had shared. Then, even though an income was not yet imperative, Sheldon wholeheartedly began looking for work. Meanwhile he suffered bouts of depression, insomnia and colitis.

When multiple problems occur simultaneously, an additional change is unwise. You can deal effectively with only one major transition at a time. It is no wonder that Sheldon's body reacted. He overloaded himself with extra decisions, responsibilities and emotional pressure. Sheldon was trying to cope with bereavement, the loss of a business and now a new job.

If you attempt too much at once, you'll probably feel overwhelmed. The stress in each change, at least in the initial stages, can seem gigantic or unmanageable. Realize this, and then treat yourself with great love and care. Pushing yourself only makes the stress increase. If at all possible, handle each issue separately until you feel somewhat more at ease—and then slowly proceed with the next. Give yourself the space to act and react without pressure. Try not to be a superperson!

Putting this into practice was quite simple for Sheldon. A short vacation gave a much-needed rest and both physical and emotional distance from his worries. He returned home with a fresh perspective. At a slower pace, Sheldon eased himself into consulting work.

Are you trying to deal with too many changes at once?

Another factor to consider is whether you are overreacting to a situaton without stopping to think. Sally is a case in point. Sally got married at age 16 in order to get away from a very critical and overbearing family. Her new husband turned out to be just as critical. Within two years Sally was a divorced mother. On the rebound, she quickly married again, but this marriage lasted only six months. The steps Sally had taken to improve her situation did not result in a better life.

Sally acted in haste, without clarifying her motivation. She runs away from difficulties instead of moving toward more promising opportunities. With time and experience, Sally might have made completely different decisions.

It is always a good idea to examine any hidden agendas. Changes made because you feel angry, jealous or rejected rarely turn out well. Feelings that are not understood can cloud your motivation and sabotage future happiness. It's best to wait until you are clearer about what you feel, what you want and why.

First give yourself a cooling-off period. Discuss your feelings calmly with a friend before you make an important decision that might have major consequences.

Another time that it isn't wise to consider a shift is when you are very depressed. If you operate out of strength rather than desperation or extreme vulnerability, you will feel more in control. Depression is to be taken seriously. However, this feeling may be an indicator of change, a symptom that something is wrong. It often precedes the decision to take a challenging step

If you are feeling somewhat depressed, I suggest that you experience your pain and live with it for a while before trying to reorder your life. Find out what is bothering you prior to taking any action. To do this, ask yourself:

• What is wrong? What is *really* bothering me? What do I want?

In order to see a way out of your gloom, consider what options are feasible.

As a final check, before making a significant change:
• Look at the number of stresses you already face.
• Clarify your feelings instead of acting hastily.
• Wait until you feel less vulnerable and can make a decision with more objectivity.
• Think about whether there is a more appropriate time to make this step.

Your Attitude Toward Fear

Although Harry had often thought about getting a divorce, he kept pretending that maintaining the marriage was really what he wanted. The problem was that at first Harry could not admit how scared he felt. "Fear isn't manly," Harry declared when I challenged him. Only when he heard other men admit to similar feelings could Harry give himself permission to be afraid.

Fear is to be expected whenever you face an unfamiliar situation. Such a reaction is common. Avoiding or ignoring fear only keeps you afraid. True bravery comes from confronting fear.

Please don't stop to question whether your worries are groundless or based upon reality, or whether other people would understand. Just try to accept the fact that you feel afraid. This will greatly expedite any changes that you are considering.

Do you have a positive attitude toward fear?
Can you generally handle your fearful feelings?

If you answered "No" be pleased that you have a starting point. From here, you can build greater self-awareness. Take credit for what you've just accomplished and trust that you can go further!

The Impact of Outside Influences

What impact have the factors mentioned in this chapter had upon your outlook?

The following exercise will help you to determine whether your social conditioning, resources, priorities, timing and attitude toward fear promote or discourage change.

Understanding Your Attitude
A Self-Test

	Promotes Change YES	Discourages Change NO
Social Conditioning		
1. Did my family background encourage independence, nonconformity and decision-making?	___	___
2. Is my present occupation supportive of change?	___	___
3. Are my friends and relatives supportive of my growth?	___	___
4. Do I know many people who have a sense of adventure and enjoy risk— or are most of the people I associate with very security-conscious?	___	___
Resources		
5. Do I have considerable experience in making similar changes?	___	___
6. Are my skills sufficient?	___	___
7. Have I all the information I need?	___	___
Priorities		
8. Is this change one that I really want?	___	___
Timing		
9. Is the timing appropriate?	___	___
Attitude Toward Fear		
10. Do I make a friend of my fear?	___	___

You are now in a much better position to effect change than you were in before reading this chapter, regardless of which items were checked. Understanding which particular factors contribute to your negative attitude toward change is the first major step in reducing their impact. This awareness is helpful because it shows you where you need to work.

If your social conditioning is unsupportive, like Yvette, you can concentrate on establishing a new social milieu. Should resources be lacking, like my career-changing and divorced clients, begin to develop new skills and obtain information. When you find that you are making changes not based upon your own priorities, it may be best to alter your plans. When the timing seems inappropriate, wait. If you are not sure just when to act, we will work on developing a better sense of your own readiness later in the book. Lastly, if fear is still a problem, the following two chapters will go into greater detail and show you how to develop a more positive attitude.

Chapter 5: Make Friends with Fear

Fear Can Be Useful

If you never feel afraid, it could be that you are taking too few risks. Fear is proof of your trying to stretch yourself beyond what is generally comfortable. It is a stage everyone goes through when taking risks.

Fear is a reliable barometer of your emotional temperature. A signal of your current lack of readiness, it informs you of the intensity of your resistance so that you'll know where to focus. When you see the problem areas, you'll be able to prepare yourself more adequately for what is ahead.

Make friends with fear and it will no longer handicap you. Adopt a positive attitude by recognizing, accepting and articulating your feelings.

There is no guarantee that if you confront fear it will immediately vanish. It probably won't right away. The chances are that you will alternate times of feeling ready to conquer the world with times of being quite unsure of yourself. The trick is to avoid being immobilized by panic whenever you are faced with anything new.

The greater your familiarity with fear, the less it will bother you. A more tolerant attitude allows you to perceive fear as a positive emotion with limitless energy that can be directed into action.

Physical Symptoms of Fear

When you are familiar with an emotion, you are consciously aware of what you are feeling at a given moment. But fear is not as easy to recognize as you might expect.

Except for the "butterflies" in your stomach, many of the physical symptoms of fear are often confused with those of anger. They include a rush of adrenalin, sweating, a flushed face, weakness in the knees, muscle tension, a dry mouth and difficulty in swallowing, exhaustion and insomnia. You may even become ill and take to your bed right before you were scheduled to try something different and risky.

Making major changes usually provokes more than one physical response. A bride at her wedding, an applicant at a job interview and a client seeing a lawyer about a divorce or legal separation will probably exhibit visible symptoms.

Think of a possible change that you're still uneasy about. What are your symptoms?

How to Recognize Fear Even When You Are Hiding It

People tend to mask their feelings in different ways because they prefer to present a much bolder image.

A student in one of my classes was helped by an analogy to become more aware of his behavior and to subsequently change it. In answer to anyone's suggestion, Quincy used the word "BUT" instead of facing his fear. A goat butts an obstacle, and Quincy was "butting" whatever he perceived as such. Quincy said "but" so often that I knew he had no time to think or feel anything. To remind Quincy of his negativism, every time he said "But...," we interrupted him and echoed "Butt." The touch of humor worked. Soon Quincy was focusing on what he was feeling instead of giving an automatic excuse.

Mattie is very much like Quincy. When faced with an alternative that might involve risk, Mattie's first response is "No." She says no to job offers, dates or help of any kind. With time and support, Mattie could look further into herself and see that her "NO" means that she is feeling anxious. When Mattie could substitute "I am frightened" for "No," she was able to examine what it was that caused her fear. This gave Mattie a more focused starting place from which to work.

When John was up for a possible promotion, his fear

took the guise of endless pacing. He also was irritable and short-tempered with his wife. In fifteeen years of marriage, Edie had learned to ask her husband whether his ire was caused by something she had done. If not, she assumed that John was only taking his own anxiety out on her.

Anyone who knew Paul well could tell by the radical change in his behavior that he was under great pressure. Normally, Paul is an easygoing person who prefers a relatively relaxed and uncrowded schedule. Before his divorce became final, Paul became restless and hyperactive. So there was no time to think about what was happening, he booked appointments back-to-back.

Other ways people mask fear are by worrying obsessively about the change, talking constantly or making endless lists that serve no apparent purpose.

Cover-Up Behavior

In which of these ways do you cover up your feelings?
- a marked change in personality or outlook _____
- misplaced anger or anger at little things _____
- repetitive use of words like "but" or "no" _____
- overscheduling, extreme restlessness _____
- incessant talking or worrying _____
- excessive list-making _____

Common Fears Associated With Change

If your excitement about a forthcoming change is overshadowed by anxiety, you don't have to live this way for very long. Become a detective. Find out what is bothering you by digging deeply into yourself. You are the only one who knows the answer to this question.

Of what am I frightened?

So that you can know what you're looking for as you probe, use the following seven fears as your foundation.

1. *Fear of The Unknown.*

Something concrete is certainly easier to face than vagueness, even if that something is unpleasant. Nothing feels worse than not knowing.

When Katie first left her job to freelance as a writer, she found herself with entirely too much time on her hands and no definite writing assignments. Katie panicked, unsure of what might happen, or when. The future looked bleak. Then a colleague sent a card that gave Katie the sense that someone else understood. In four words, a simple message crystalized exactly what Katie was feeling. The card read, "Welcome to the void."

Tension mounts when you don't know what to expect, if something will actually occur, or how long you'll have to wait. What creates even greater anxiety is knowing that the outcome of a situation is largely out of your control. Imagine how you would feel if you were waiting for the verdict in a child custody case, a large insurance claim, a driving test or your doctoral orals.

A fear of the unknown is to be expected in a world where no one has a crystal ball with which to predict the future. People learn to accept the fact that they must live with a degree of uncertainty. Perhaps, after all, certainty is only an illusion.

You can get a better perspective by realizing that nothing stays the way it is for very long. Whatever you are feeling anxious about today will eventually be yesterday's history.

2. *Fear of The Consequences of Your Actions*

After placing an ad in the newspaper for a sewing workshop, Phyllis became jittery. "Perhaps I'll get too many phone calls. More than ten people won't fit into my tiny apartment at one time. I will have to schedule another class, but how can I, with no other free evening? What will I do?"

When Charlie began researching possible career fields, he compiled a list of ten people to call for information about their work. This was as far as Charlie was willing to go. He balked at setting up any appointments. "I'm afraid that someone might offer me a job when I know I'm not ready to make a decision."

Both Phyllis and Charlie were afraid that if they took even one small step toward making a change, something terrible would happen. They took the path of least resistance and did nothing.

Try to be more specific when you're anticipating dire consequences of a change. What is the worst that you can imagine?

Reality is never as bad as we imagine. The worst that Phyllis might have to face is an overflow of students. If that were the case, she could always start a waiting list for future classes. It's not too likely that Charlie will receive a job offer so soon. However, if he did, Charlie could always say no.

3. *Fear of Failure or Success.*

The fear of failure and the fear of success are two sides of the same issue.

Samantha often complains about her second marriage, but does nothing else. She feels unsure about her husband's love since he is very critical. Because Samantha sees ending another marriage as proof of her personal failure, she believes that the only alternative is to stay.

Samantha is deluding herself. Clinging to an unhappy relationship can be as much a failure as leaving.

Remember that giving yourself permission to fail makes room for possible success. However, achieving your goals can be equally frightening.

Katie, the freelance writer, began to get articles published. Then she was offered a contract for a book. As she progressed, Katie worried that this book might turn out to be a best seller. She was so used to struggling for recognition that the thought of finally being in a better position was too much to bear.

Success can make you feel inadequate. Katie's self-image has not kept up with her recent accomplishments. She may still see herself as a woman without talent, confidence or the ability to earn considerable income. She worries, "If this book succeeds, then I will have to write an even better one next time!"

Katie is putting herself on a treadmill where perpetual achievement is a requirement for personal happiness. Success is only relative to whomever perceives it, and it doesn't last forever. To avoid getting caught in this snag, put your focus on the *process* rather than on the *results* of your efforts.

4. *Fear of Making The Wrong Choice.*

Josie had just started a new job which she was quite pleased about. It offered her a higher salary and more room for advancement than the previous position. However, because Josie wanted to make certain that she was not missing out on better opportunities, she set up several other job interviews. Each time Josie had an appointment, the new position seemed enticing. After ten prospective jobs, Josie became very confused.

Josie assumed that there were right and wrong choices to make. She probably could have continued presenting herself with new possibilities forever. There is no one perfect job, lover, apartment, or choice. At some point, without knowing what is just around the corner, you may as well pick one. Get as much information as you need to make a decision, without worrying about making the wrong one.

You don't have to be all-wise. Allow yourself the space to make a mistake, change your mind, or try another alternative.

5. *Fear of Commitment.*

This fear is another aspect of the fear of making the wrong choice.

Louise is very much like Josie. When she went looking for an apartment, Louise found one that suited her perfectly. Her salary was high enough to cover the rent, the neighborhood was safe, the rooms were fairly large. The only problem was the required two-year lease. "Perhaps I'll only need it for a year. I might get a job in another town, or be married by then. How can I possibly commit myself to a two-year lease when I don't know what's going to happen?"

Louise's anxiety was based upon her assumption that

any decision was irrevocable. A commitment to Louise was a choice that locked her in forever. She never considered other options. For example, a sublease arrangement might have taken the pressure off. Renting an apartment now does not preclude altering one's plans later.

6. *Fear Of Rejection.*
Amanda would like to return to work but worries that her husband won't approve. She keeps silent but builds up resentment about lost opportunities.

Greg and Sophie have lived together for ten years in silent collusion. Sophie has never raised her voice or shown anger even though she has often felt furious. Greg wishes his wife were more assertive. He'd enjoy having her stand up to him when he is unfair. Greg has not yet expressed his frustration concerning Sophie's complaint behavior.

If neither person in a marriage is willing to risk for fear of losing the other's love, they perpetuate a boring, non-growth relationship. Amanda, Greg and Sophie would not think of attempting to do anything that might test their spouse's loyalty. They were all so busy worrying about being rejected that the possibility of their partners feeling the same way never crossed anyone's mind.

7. *Fear of Loneliness.*
Morton considers divorcing his wife, but hesitates. The thought of endless dinners alone next to a telephone which never rings frightens him. Morton is not willing to risk leaving an unhappy situation for a potentially less happy one. He envisions long periods of loneliness and despair.

Loneliness is not the only result of being alone. Solitude can also be useful. Morton will require considerable time in solitude for thinking, feeling, planning and dreaming.

If he divorces, Morton will probably find that his changed status causes new problems. He may feel that he has little in common with his married friends. Alliances do not develop immediately. Therefore, Morton may feel temporarily isolated.

Any major life change is at first lonely. However, the

experience can help you to discover your inner resources, reach out to others and eventually form close relationships.

Because they overlap, you may have difficulty distinguishing between these seven fears. All that is important is that you become more aware of your feelings. This understanding facilitates your moving beyond fear.

Self-Defeating Behavior

People in a period of transition often create obstacles for themselves. A symptom of fear, their self-defeating behavior serves as a protection. By blocking change, it maintains the status quo. This is where they feel safe.

Do you want fear to get the best of you? If not, look more closely at your behavior and the purposes it serves. No one ever gets rid of feelings by pretending that they don't exist. Consider fear an ally rather than a dictator or an enemy. Instead of fighting fear, try to understand it.

The following examples will help you to identify your own behavior. Since this behavior is the same for men and women, the descriptions alternate gender.

Can you recognize any of these traits in yourself?

• *I don't usually take responsibility for myself or my decisions.*

Instead of making overtures to rectify what is wrong with his life, this individual would rather wait for the telephone to ring or solutions to appear by themselves. He hopes that someone else will save him, take care of him or seek him out without his having to lift a finger.

By assuming that other people can right all wrongs, he puts them on a pedestal and gives away all his power.

The person who avoids taking responsibility for himself may also blame others for what happens to him. Here, the basic assumption is that things would be very different "if only I had . . . a husband, wife, more money, a kinder boss, a better job, etc." Remember the Victim Syndrome which we discussed earlier? A passive role is much preferred to making a commitment, doing the hard work or spending the time and energy to improve a situation.

- *My expectations are extremely high or low.*

A person with a glorified image of herself and others believes that success is imminent. She will achieve all goals with no snags. She assumes that other people will always be there in a supportive way. She says to herself, "I'm so terrific that I can do anything. And everyone will applaud me, help me, like me." With such high standards, she is frequently disappointed. She rarely takes into consideration the fact that people have weaknesses, problems and feelings, or needs different from hers.

The person who resigns herself to a humdrum life is the opposite. She is sure that "No one will offer me assistance. They don't really care. I'm not very smart, so I'd better not try." In a self-fulfilling prophecy, she anticipates being disappointed by others or failing. Satisfied with getting very little out of life, she does not compete, develop her potential or risk much.

Reality is somewhere in the middle of these two positions. No one is totally interesting, powerful, intelligent or flawless—or inept, disorganized, uncooperative or unpopular!

- *I lack confidence.*

Without a sense of self-worth, this individual feels doomed to failure. Any past successes are quickly forgotten, any assets discounted.

Some messages are deeply entrenched.

"I can't."

"I'm no good. I am a failure."

"I'm sure that everyone else is much, much further ahead, more capable, active, intelligent, assertive than I."

- *I am overly self-critical.*

Instead of praise for even trying, this person constantly whips himself for what wasn't accomplished. When he is most in need of support, he gets angry at being less than perfect.

He makes endless comparisons with others. Singling out only his weaknesses, he forgets that he also has strengths.

Typical statements are:

"I always mess things up."

"Oh, I am so fat."

"Look at the way I just served that ball. It landed in the court next to ours."

- *I cater to others and deny my own needs and wishes.*

She is the helper, nurturer, confidante. Used to a position of servitude, she puts everyone else first. The needs of her children, mate, parents, friends or employer are certainly more important than her own. In fact, she is so busy taking care of others that she probably doesn't even know what she wants. If anyone asks her, she promptly replies without thinking, "I don't know. I don't care. It's not really that important."

- *I live in the past.*

A person who lives in the past finds planning for the future very difficult. The present goes unnoticed. Opportunities disappear because they make no impact. The past is like a magnet.

Caught in a time machine, such an individual utters sentences that start like this:

"If only I had...."

"I could have been...."

"My life has been so hard...."

"My marriage was so perfect that....."

- *I try to anticipate and control the future by preparing for all contingencies.*

Feeling insecure about the future, this person tries to predict the outcome of all present efforts. Endless planning and rushes of anxiety interfere with his spontaneity and pleasure in the moment.

His constant preoccupation with the next moment keeps him sufficiently out of this one.

Common ruminations are:

"If I do ..., then ... will happen."

"I want guarantees that it will work out. What insurance against any pitfalls can I create?"

Yet no matter what he anticipates, something he didn't think of always happens!

- *I intellectualize instead of acting.*

This individual lives more in his head than anywhere else. He is very analytical: examining causes, solutions and alternatives. The constant use of cliches and jargon means that he sometimes gets lost in his words.

He talks a blue streak about what he plans on doing, makes excuses, but does little. Such verbal activity enables him to keep his dreams alive. Perhaps he prefers not to risk losing them by carrying them out in action.

Typical comments are:

"When I get my act together...."

"It's my insecurity complex that prevents me...."

"I am sure that my paranoia and separation anxiety coupled with the trauma of losing my brother...."

"I wonder why I always seem to...."

"I don't want to hurt you, but...."

- *I am very impatient.*

Time is rapidly passing. Yesterday is too late.

For a person who feels very pressured, only immediate gratification will do.

Her conversation is filled with such phrases as:

"It's too late."

"I must do it by ... or else ..."

"I'm getting older."

"I'll give myself one week."

She is in a panic about this change because of a lack of awareness of her own rhythm. Such impatience masks a lack of readiness.

- *I don't believe that I deserve to be happy.*

This individual somehow always manages to find the one cloud in an otherwise sunny sky. Because life seems to be a perpetual struggle against unfair odds, he is often tired.

Happiness is a risk he is not willing to take, because it may not last. Conditioned to frustration and dashed hopes, he has a low tolerance for success or joy. He resigns himself to getting less than he really wants.

You will hear him say things like:

"I'm feeling great but I don't know how long it will last."

- *I either see too many or too few options.*

The person who sees too many options feels that the entire world is at her doorstep. However, her priorities are unclear.

Overwhelmed by so many choices, she will fret:

"I don't know what to do. I can't decide. It's too confusing."

"I don't know what I want. I only know what I don't want."

The person with the opposite problem feels boxed in because no alternatives seem viable. She simply finds a reason to dismiss them all.

Her statements reduce possibilities.

"No. I don't like that."

"There's nothing out there for me."

"It's a bad time for jobs. There's a recession."

"I'm stuck here."

"No one suits me."

- *I see everything in absolutes.*

This person sees the world in extremes with only either-or choices. There are no grays in his landscape. Decisions for him are very difficult to make.

He pressures himself with statements like these.

"It has to be."

"There's really nothing else I can do."

"If I don't do this, I'll be worse off than if I stayed where I am now."

- *I avoid problems by sweeping them under the rug.*

It is much easier for this person to ignore problems than to face them. Confronting the unpleasant reality of her situation might mean having to do something about it. She is not ready to make this effort.

Instead, when her friends express concern about signals they notice, she insists:

"Everything is fine."

"There's nothing wrong."

"I'm very happy."

"I'm just feeling under the weather today. It's a cold coming on."

- *I put off making a decision or taking a step—indefinitely.*

Although very aware of his need to make a change, this person procrastinates. The task seems so insurmountable that somehow he never manages even to take the first step.

He gives himself many excuses.

"Tomorrow."
"Maybe when I am more motivated."
"I will, soon."
• *I feel like an imposter, trying on a role that doesn't suit me.*

This individual may have recently made a dramatic change quite successfully, but feels very uncomfortable.

Perhaps the change was made too quickly for her to integrate this new role or self-image. Everyone is applauding and assumes she is where she wants to be. Yet, in spite of these accomplishments, she feels as though she were still a very tiny child.

Silently, she whispers to herself:
"If they ever found out how I really felt. . . ."

It is not unusual for a person deep in the throes of a major transition to temporarily exhibit self-defeating behavior. In time, with more awareness so that you can catch yourself in the act, you will reverse this negative thinking. The first step in changing your attitude is recognizing it.

In what ways is your own behavior typical of a person blocking change?

To find out if you are maintaining the status quo by a negative attitude, please fill in the following chart.

A Fearful Outlook: A Self-Test

	Yes	No
1. Do I prefer to blame others for what happens to me instead of taking the responsibility for my own life?	___	___
2. Are my expectations unrealistic?	___	___
3. Do I lack confidence in my abilities?	___	___
4. Do I continually criticize myself for what I didn't do or did badly?	___	___
5. Do I deny the importance of my own needs and wishes? Do I think of others before I think of myself?	___	___
6. Do I live in the past more than in the moment? Do I miss opportunities because I don't notice them?	___	___

	Yes	No
7. Do I feel unprepared for whatever happens? Am I so busy overplanning and anticipating the next minute that I lose sight of this one?	___	___
8. Do I analyze my behavior, make excuses and feel guilty for what I didn't do? Do I use cliches, jargon and then get lost in my own words?	___	___
9. Am I very impatient, feeling that yesterday is too late?	___	___
10. Am I afraid to be happy?	___	___
11. Do I find it difficult to narrow down or expand my alternatives?	___	___
12. Am I unable to see a middle ground?	___	___
13. Do I ignore problems?	___	___
14. Am I often a procrastinator?	___	___
15. Am I uncomfortable in a new image or role? Am I afraid of being found out?	___	___

A majority of "yes" answers usually means that your attitude needs some improvement. However, this is no cause for dismay. In fact, quite the reverse is true. Such insight is a considerable accomplishment that works in your favor. Your responses to the questions on the chart provide you with detailed information about how you get in your own way. As a result, you're likely to be more in charge of your behavior and much less immobilized by fear.

All of my clients are at first reluctant to confront their fearful feelings. They anticipate that it will make them more anxious. After we talk about the various ways in which people exhibit fear, and how they can identify their own specific worries, my clients are pleased to discover that they have a higher tolerance for fear. Articulating fear helped them to quickly feel more able to cope with it.

Any task seems more feasible after recognizing and understanding the origin and scope of your fear. The next step is to learn how to channel your feelings.

Part Three: Turnaround and Momentum

Chapter 6:
Redirecting Negativity

Take Advantage of Fear

After several months of unemployment, Sydelle's funds were diminishing. She found looking for a job especially discouraging. On the days that interviews were scheduled, if she awoke feeling anxious, Sydelle would sometimes cancel her appointment. However, this behavior only created new worries and guilt. "I wish I could dig out the roots of my fear and throw it away," Sydelle declared.

Treating fear as a problematic, undesirable separate entity is an unconstructive attitude. It would be better to accept and embrace the part of yourself that is scared. This allows you to function as a whole, integrated person.

Fear is a source of energy which can either be invested in maintaining the status quo, or channelled into selected action. Considerable energy is wasted in the effort to hold yourself back.

It's a good idea to be less serious about your struggles. A sense of humor allows you to laugh at yourself when you feel most shaky. Laughter relaxes tension, adds a broader perspective and shifts your focus away from pain. Had Sydelle taken her anxiety less seriously, she might have felt more positive about everything.

If fear is to be utilized as a valuable resource, it must be channelled. Here's a systematic strategy for channelling your fear into action.

First think of a specific change you wish to accomplish but also fear. Then *acknowledge the fact that you are afraid.* Understand that you won't be scared forever.

Accept your feelings even if you don't like them. Give

90 *Change*

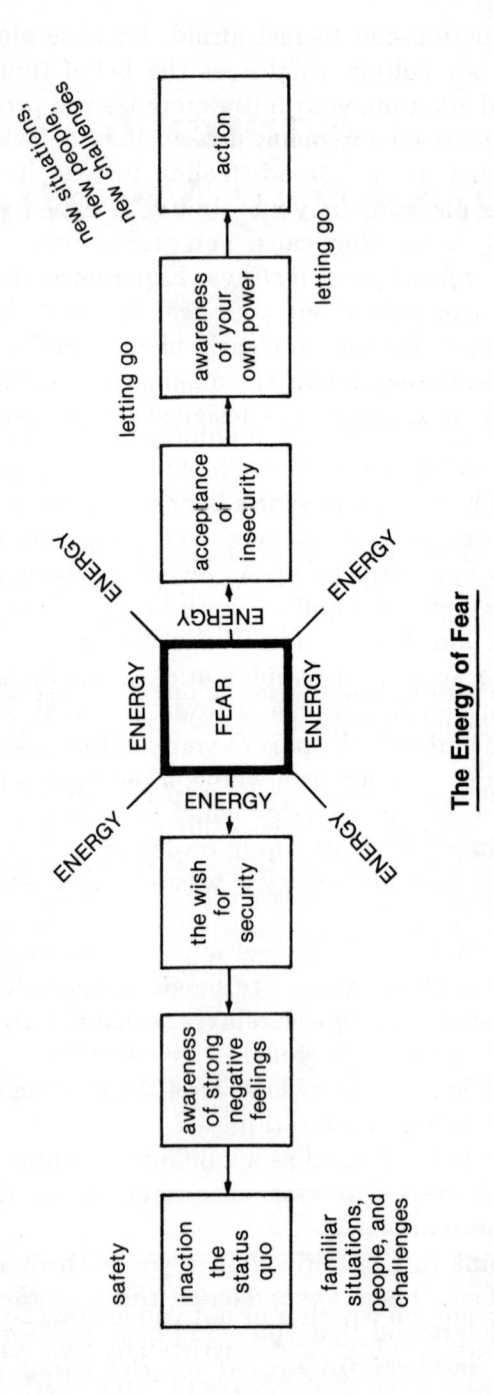

The Energy of Fear

Flow diagram centered on a "FEAR" box with "ENERGY" radiating in eight directions.

Downward chain (leading to safety / familiar situations, people, and challenges):
- the wish for security
- awareness of strong negative feelings
- inaction / the status quo

Upward chain (leading via "letting go" to new situations, new people, new challenges):
- acceptance of insecurity
- awareness of your own power
- action

yourself permission to feel afraid. Because almost everything in our culture reinforces the belief that fear is an unwanted emotion, your initial impulse will probably be to chastise yourself for being jittery. It is pointless to fight against what you are already feeling. Instead, if you possibly can, take pleasure in your ability to experience intense emotions, even if they cause you discomfort.

Now *confront your feelings.* Experience them so fully that you can talk about your fear in great detail. Name specific fears. Be able to clearly identify and verbalize the negative statements you are making in a silent inner dialogue. The next exercise is designed for this purpose.

Worry Beads

Worry Beads is an offshoot of Red Flags. It helps you to isolate your fears and self-defeating behavior.

First picture yourself achieving a specific goal. Then ask yourself:

- What am I afraid of happening if I make this change?
- What am I telling myself about the consequences of this action?
- What negative messages do I give myself which conveniently stop me from proceeding?

If you have forgotten them, look over the list of fears and self-defeating behavior presented in the last chapter. For *each* goal you are considering, fill in this chart:

Use "I" statements when completing the right-hand column.

Preliminary Goal	What stops me? What negative messages do I tell myself?
1)	a. b. c. d. etc.

So you can tell whether or not you are on the right track, here is a sample chart. It was written by a woman returning to work after a maternity leave of three years.

Preliminary Goal	What stops me? What negative messages do I tell myself?
1) Find a good job in banking	a. I'm too old. b. I'm not qualified. c. No one will hire me. d. I'll have no income. We won't be able to afford anything. e. If I do find a job, I am sure I won't like it. f. I'll leave and have to look for work again.

Add as many messages as you are aware of to your own list. Be persistent. Throughout the next few days, focus on what you are feeling. Any time you experience any anxiety, applaud! Congratulate yourself both for being honest and for making the effort to articulate what isn't always fully conscious. After verbalizing your fears, you will discover that they seem less threatening.

Everyone feels better knowing that other people go through the same tribulations. Mutual commiseration can be very rewarding. To provide the opportunity for this, meet with a friend on a regular basis and talk about your fears. You might also talk with someone who has recently taken the step you're considering. By discussing mutual feelings, and hearing someone else's experiences and strategies, you'll get a more realistic picture of what is ahead. If you are changing your career, look for people who landed the kind of job you think you want. Should a divorce be on your mind, find someone who is happy living alone. Seek positive models who are willing to discuss their own hesitations and the time it took them to overcome their fears.

Identify whatever you must give up in order to reach this goal: a self-concept, attitude, role or type of behavior. Making a change is a form of giving birth to a new way of being. Before you can adopt a new self-image, role or lifestyle, you must let go of the previous one. Giving up a long familiar part of your life is not a simple feat. It isn't really a question of whether this part of your life gave you pleasure or pain. What is important is that you have grown accustomed to having it around.

Mourn your loss. Mourning involves both acknowledging a loss and taking ample time to let go. It confirms the importance to you of a particular part of your life.

Mourning

The purpose of this exercise is to help you identify exactly what it is that you're letting go of by choice. It also shows you how to clarify your loss and be more open to the change.

Look at your fantasy of succcess. Then ask:
- What must I give up to make this change?

Now say goodbye to each characteristic, role, behavior, circumstance or belief that seems appropriate. Your Worry Beads can help you to begin. The following chart is based on the responses of the women in the last exercise.

Mourning

What I want to say goodbye to	In order to say hello to
Feeling too old	Feeling youthful and vigorous
Feeling unqualified	Being competent
Lacking confidence	Being confident
Being fearful about money	Feeling financially successful
Being negative	Being enthusiastic and optimistic
Dreading the future	Looking forward to tomorrow

Mourning requires patience. It should be practical before, during and after the time a change is made.

Review your strengths for coping (Chapter 2).

You have just practiced two that you will find especially helpful:
- able to face my fears
- able to accept them

A third strength is the next logical one to work on:
- able to act in spite of my fears.

Test reality in small doses. Instead of trying to do everything at once, focus on simple tasks which can be accomplished even if you are feeling scared. It's important to build up a record of success for yourself, so your confidence increases.

Test The Water

To me, confronting my fear is often a joyous experience. Let me give you an example. Although I used to be a fair swimmer, I was never really comfortable in the water. In fact, I always dreaded getting my face wet. Two years ago, I decided that I would take lessons. When the instructor asked me to blow bubbles with my head in the water, I realized that I was terrified. I couldn't see, hear or trust that the world existed. However, I was determined to learn and gradually conquered my fear. Soon I could travel thirty laps and swim underwater as well.

It's time to test the water. Select an easily manageable task that can be accomplished in a few minutes. I didn't swim in one lesson. First I had to practice putting my head in the water for the count of ten. Gradually, I could stay in longer without going into an absolute panic.

What can you think of to do?

Here are a few examples.

If you are seeking work, make one telephone call, set up an appointment, and go to the library for information about possible career opportunities.

If you're thinking of leaving your marriage, check into available lawyers, the divorce laws in your state, and existing support groups. Talk to one person who is already divorced.

If you are not ready to talk to anyone just yet, make a deal with yourself. Write a note on your calendar for a particular day to place the preliminary call—and be sure to follow your memo.

Place your emphasis on your attempt rather than on a successful outcome. It does not matter whether you get rejected or put your worst foot forward. What counts is that you made an effort. Be sure to take credit for this. Reward yourself for your efforts. (Review Gold Stars.)

Experience your feelings, but don't let them stop you. Realize that although you won't be at your best, you can still function effectively. Other people won't notice your sweating palms or shaking knees.

You'll feel great pride in yourself when you don't allow anxiety to get the best of you. Handling yourself with composure when you're shaky has a delightful effect; you will forget how scared you were!

Allow yourself the time to integrate the change and overcome any remaining fears. In the beginning, when you're still in unfamiliar territory, anticipate a reaction of fear and learn to live with it. It's okay to be a person who is sometimes afraid. Stage fright can help you to stay on your toes so that you perform better.

Give yourself ample time to experience your feelings in many new activities. Overcome fear and build confidence gradually through repeated exposure.

You can look forward to a brighter tomorrow. I've observed an interesting phenomenon in my own life which is encouraging. Once, many years ago, fear was a great nuisance to me. It caused me considerable frustration and self-hate. Now, after years of extensive risk-taking, fear never shows its face before I act. First I venture out, and only much later, if at all, do any doubts arise.

So start today with tiny steps. The more times you take risks, the more confident you'll feel and the less fear will get in your way.

The following diagram summarizes what we're covered in this chapter:

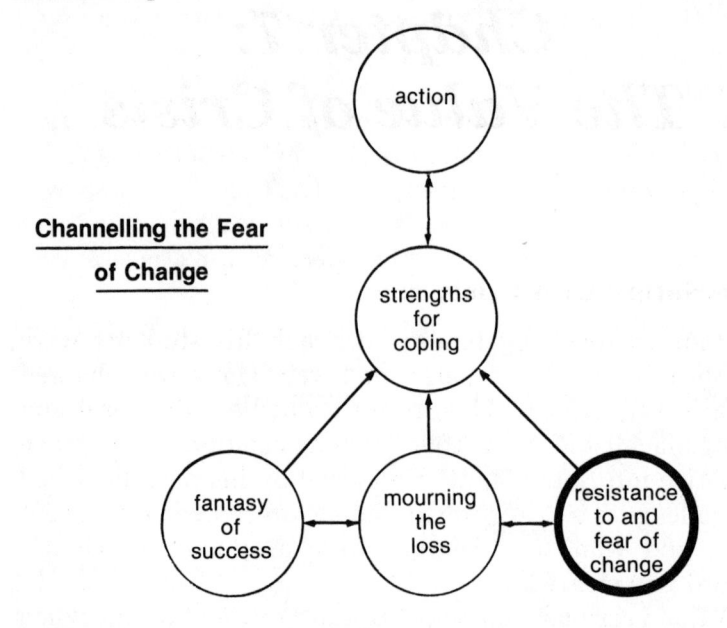

Channelling the Fear of Change

```
                    action
                      ↕
                  strengths
                     for
                   coping
                   ↗  ↑  ↖
            fantasy  mourning  resistance
              of  ←   the   ←   to and
            success    loss     fear of
                                change
```

Go over this procedure as often as necessary to increase your assurance. *Trust your own capability and power.* Believe that you possess adequate resources for accomplishing your fondest dreams. And you do, for one of your most valuable assets is fear. So take advantage of it!

Chapter 7: The Value of Crisis

The Nature Of A Crisis

Prior to receiving tenure, although his students were highly motivated and performed well, Hank was charged with incompetency. This meant immediate dismissal and being blacklisted from other teaching positions. Such grave injustice infuriated Hank. Energized by his rage, he asked his colleagues to testify on his behalf, presented an excellent case, and won. The charges were dropped and Hank's record was cleared.

A flood seriously damaged Susan's office at a time when she was rather short of funds and just beginning to build a therapy practice. Susan was upset because the condition of the office made it necessary to cancel or postpone all appointments indefinitely. Her income had ceased. Clients had to wait. The insurance company procrastinated about making a settlement. Susan didn't know what to do about the fact that she had, at least for the present, lost control of her life. A week passed and Susan began to develop chest pains. She had difficulty breathing. Not being able to stand this delay any longer, Susan made the decision to purchase new wall-to-wall carpeting at her own expense. Her action accelerated a satisfactory resolution. Within a few days, Susan received a rather sizable check from her broker.

Hank and Susan were both confronted with an outside event which interrupted their normal daily routines, threatened their well-being and temporarily altered the course of their lives. How do you think you would react if you were in their places?

In a crisis situation, shock and dismay usually provoke an initial response of helplessness. Typical thoughts are:
"Why did this have to happen?"
"Am I being punished for something I did wrong?"
"Who will take care of me?"
"How can I possibly manage?"

Fear is rarely an issue in an emergency, because when you are so busy focusing on what to do next, there is no time to think about anything else. Anxieties either disappear or become less of a priority. You know that it would be foolish to crumble and allow the situation to get the best of you. Somehow you must pull yourself together and cope.

If you were faced with an emergency tomorrow, what would you do first? Suppose:

- your son were arrested
- the doctor informed you of the necessity for immediate surgery
- a fire completely destroyed your new home
- you suffered a financial reversal
- a loved relative were to die
- your apartment were burglarized
- the river overflowed and you must evacuate the town
- you were terminated from your job

In these situations, where would you put your energy?
Think of a recent crisis you have experienced.
What were your immediate feelings?
How did you cope?
What was the impact of this crisis on the rest of your life? Consider how it changed your present circumstance and future plans.

Crisis As A Changemaker

Certainly no one consciously seeks an unpleasant or problematic situation. Yet we must remember that although it is upsetting, any crisis is a stimulus for growth. Here is fertile ground for building your ego strength. This is possible because a crisis crystalizes, exaggerates and highly accelerates change. People who weather a crisis effectively go through certain stages. They:

- act in spite of fear
- tap inner resources of which they were unaware in the past
- accept a loss
- evaluate their self-image, role and lifestyle
- choose the direction in which they want to go next

This is the sequence of events:

100 *Change*

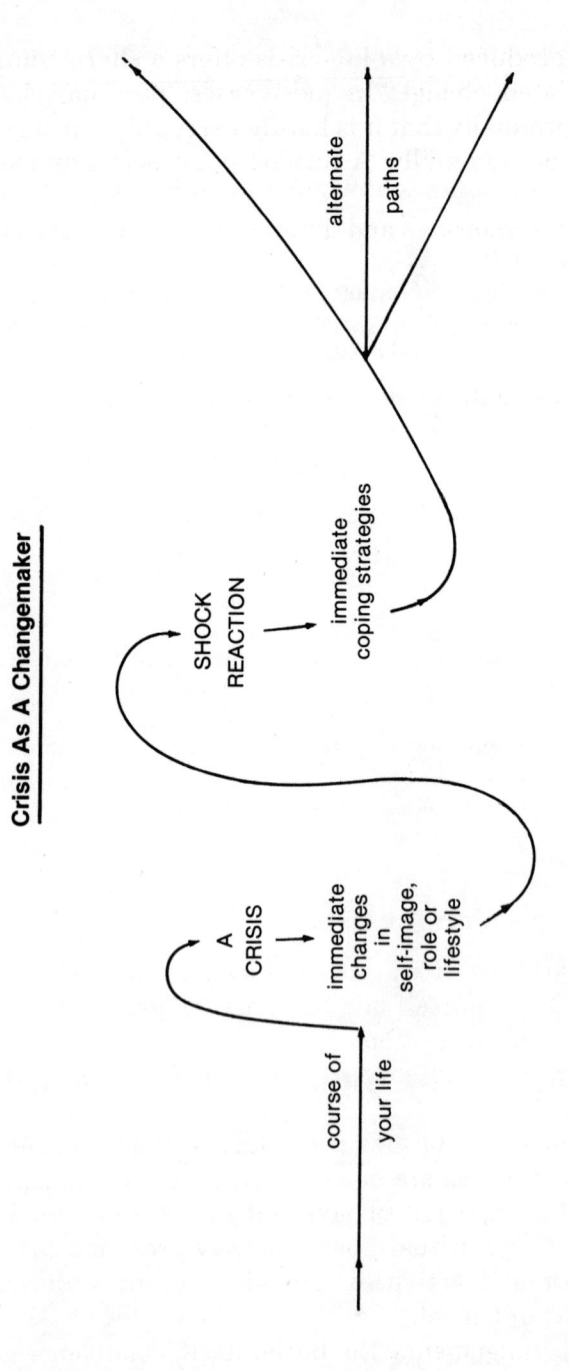

Crisis As A Changemaker

course of your life → A CRISIS → immediate changes in self-image, role or lifestyle → SHOCK REACTION → immediate coping strategies → alternate paths

Change produced by a life-crisis offers a sharp contrast to self-initiated change. In most cases, personal change evolves so gradually that it is hardly perceptible. In a crisis, transitions occur rapidly. A turning point is clearly identifiable.

For other similarities and differences, examine the chart that follows.

Crisis And Change

Change Produced By A Crisis	Self-Initiated Change
sudden	gradual
dramatic	sometimes imperceptible
rapid	slow
creates problems	solves problems
causes a reaction	a result of action
no choice is involved	requires a conscious decision
unexpected	anticipated
unplanned	planned
disruptive: upsets daily routines	routines can be designed to facilitate change
no time for fear	fear in anticipation

creates some upheaval
involves a loss
requires strength and coping strategies
alters the direction of your life

How To Cope With A Crisis

In order to learn from this experience, you must first be able to manage yourself and the crisis. To show you how, here are several suggestions:

Follow whatever rituals are associated with this particular crisis.

A ritual is an established procedure to follow on certain occasions. When you are in a crisis, it is very comforting to know what is expected of you and not to have to think about what to do. Rituals, because they prescribe customary behavior and activities, provide continuity during a time of great upheaval.

Funeral arrangements, the burial itself, condolence calls

and definite mourning periods help the bereaved to deal with a recent death.

When your spouse suddenly deserts you, there are several useful distractions: the selection of a lawyer, figuring out your finances, preparing your legal case and deciding when to file for divorce.

If you are the victim of a serious accident or illness, hospital administrative and medical procedures provide a tangible footing and regularity which counteract your uncertainty and stress.

For those in the midst of a job transition, writing a resume, planning a job-hunting campaign and setting up interviews give a meaningful focus and direction. Though less clearly delineated and requiring more initiative than other rituals, these procedures can be very absorbing.

What rituals have been established for the situation you are now facing?

Involve yourself in daily routines and chores.

Many activities can substitute for rituals.

Chris was left with four small childen when his wife died after a year's bout with cancer. A job, thirteen cats, two dogs, an acre of land, a house, twelve loads of laundry each week and cooking meals for his hungry youngsters gave Chris an organized routine to follow. "There was no one to help me. It was all rather hectic and monotonous. I didn't have the time to think, so I just put one foot in front of the other."

Liz, my mother, was widowed abruptly at age sixty-four, after forty-two years of marriage. The details of ending a family business, finances, insurance, meetings with an attorney, accountant and the bank kept her quite gainfully occupied for the first few months after the funeral.

To set a structure and provide order in a temporarily chaotic life, continue set routines. These include: reading the paper, walking your dog, feeding the cat, buying groceries, planning and cooking meals, doing household chores, playing a regular tennis game, jogging in the morning, taking your child to school and going to work.

Acknowledge your loss(es).

Each crisis involves a particular kind of loss. Understanding the nature of your loss makes coping with it much easier.

The Kinds Of Losses In Each Crisis

Bereavement Desertion	⟶ Loss of Love Loss of Security Loss of Status
Accident and Illness	⟶ Loss of Health and Mobility Loss of Independence
Burglary Flood Fire	⟶ Loss of Security
Unemployment	⟶ Loss of Structure Loss of Status Loss of Security
Financial Reversal	⟶ Loss of Security Loss of Status

The Loss of Love. Love is a basic human need. When it is lost, you feel alone and vulnerable. It is then difficult to believe in the order of the universe and to remain open to future involvements. As a result of the loss of love, you may become withdrawn, hostile, depressed or frightened. Planned changes involving the loss of love are divorce, separation and the end of an intimate relationship.

The Loss of Health and Mobility. Health and mobility are generally taken for granted until they are missing. Helplessness, a loss of independence and normal functioning may produce anger, fear, extreme self-protectiveness, depression or apathy.

The Loss of Security and Status. A sense of security comes from being in a familiar home and work environment, with established routines. Security is lost when your home is invaded by natural forces or a criminal act, you are terminated from your job, suffer a financial reversal or end a relationship. Something or someone you counted on is suddenly gone. Status comes from having a role, position or place in the world. You are a husband, wife, parent, son, daughter, employer, employee, with an income and reputation. Without this safe niche and comfortable self-definition, you may feel like an outsider.

The Loss of Structure. Work provides not only status and security but also a way of structuring your time. Unemployment can leave you feeling disoriented, depressed, ashamed of your recent idleness. Time hangs heavily when your priorities are unclear and you are unmotivated. Without a job, you may feel unfocused, unimportant and at loose ends.

What specific losses are you experiencing now?

Allow yourself a period of mourning.

After acknowledging a loss, take the time to grieve by practicing the exercise Mourning. (For a review of this exercise, see Chapter 5.) Here are several suggestions for how to mourn in specific crisis situations.

Mourning In A Crisis

Crisis Situation	Say Goodbye To (Loss)	Say Hello To
Desertion and Bereavement	Companionship	Being alone
	The security of being in a steady relationship	Vulnerability and self-reliance
	Trusting	Feeling betrayed or cautious
	Loving	Anger and fear
Accident and Illness	Independence	Dependence
	Freedom of movement	Limitations and self-protectiveness
	Taking the future for granted	Uncertainty about the future
	Lack of awareness of your body	Extreme awareness of your body
	Unlimited energy	Being tired, conserving energy

Crisis Situation	Say Goodbye To	Say Hello To
Burglary	Complacency	Uneasiness
	Feeling secure and safe	Anxiety, fear and anger
Unemployment	A steady income	Uncertain funds
	A sense of belonging	Feeling isolated
	A place to go every day	Having no clear destination
	Feeling useful	Idleness
	Having little leisure	Owning your time
	A clear identity	An uncertain role
Financial reversal	Sufficient funds	Anxiety about money
	Confidence in your own judgment	Self-doubt

After some time elapses, it may be possible for you to move on to another stage. This depends upon how ready you feel. Look at the first item on the chart: say goodbye to companionship and hello to being alone. When you are more comfortable with being alone, you will be able to let go of solitude and again accept companionship.

You may be wondering how much time you will need to mourn before this happens. Mourning periods are not uniform in length. Neither are they necessarily continuous. People take a loss differently, according to its relevance, their age, prior experience and personality.

Barbara Hunter Getz mourns before a relationship has actually ended. When Barbara was thirty-six and divorced, she nursed her dying father. This is Barbara's perspective on mourning, taken from our conversations and her unpublished journal:

"As soon as I know I am losing a person, I begin to let go. I accept the loss so that I have a shorter mourning period. I've learned that the harder it is for me to open to a loss, the longer I will grieve. (So) I lived his dying at the time.

Mourning is not a constant state. It comes and goes. I always thought of it as a state one entered, never to know relief until the necessary weeks or months or years had passed which enabled the mourner to shed that phase, that role.... Instead, I've found many rays of brightness...along the way ... and ... the pain ... can recede from moment to moment...just as all rhythms in nature ebb and flow."

If you were recently in a crisis, ask yourself:

How long have I mourned this loss?

Schedule regular periods of solitude.

Time alone gives you the space to take stock of recent events, experience your feelings without pressure, absorb and accept your circumstances, and think about what you want to do.

When Noel's teenage son was killed in an automobile accident, solitude became an absolute imperative. "I learned to cherish scheduling time alone after Leroy died. I went away by myself just to remember him, to talk to myself, to cry, to shout and face the fact that he was gone."

Solitude can heal sensitive wounds caused by the loss of a job, lover, your health, income or property. Therefore, I suggest that you dedicate at least a half hour each day to your well-being and recovery.

How much time do you spend alone for this purpose?

Clarify your priorities.

A crisis shrinks your world so only the immediate moment is relevant. You stop thinking about tomorrow, the quality of your life or personal satisfaction. Instead, issues of survival take precedence: personal health and safety, sleep, food, a place to live, adequate money.

When you are busy mopping up the flood in your basement, all that is on your mind is preserving your home. If you are out of funds, a social life becomes less of a priority than looking for a job or figuring out how to pay the rent.

Decide what is most important and deal with that first. Prioritizing brings back order in a time of upheaval.

To give focus to your day, pose three questions each morning:

- What details must I address immediately?
- Which ones are least pressing and can be postponed?

- How can I best use my time and energy today?

Gather whatever information you need to cope more successfully with this situation.
Take nothing for granted. Ask questions, read, collect data, get legal assistance when it is appropriate. Use this information to increase your options.

For instance, if you are incapacitated, ask your physician about your physical condition, chances for recovery and alternate treatments. If you just received an eviction notice, find out what your rights are as a tenant.

The questions to ask are:
- What information do I lack?
- Where can I get it?

Solicit support.
Why try to cope alone with a difficult situation? Perhaps you have friends and relatives who are eager to help. People like to feel needed. They can give you reassurance, advice, time, professional resources and sometimes money. There are often programs, agencies and self-help groups set up especially for those who are bereaved, deserted, abused, the victims of crime, homeless, unemployed or otherwise indigent. Some of them are even free or at a minimal cost.

What kind of assistance are you seeking?

Accept your current circumstances even though you may not like them.

Since you cannot erase what has happened, you may as well resign yourself. There is certainly no point in resisting reality. Instead, consider yourself as a person in the midst of a transition. Reexamine the future in terms of the present. Ask:
- How has my life changed as a result of this crisis?
- What plans can I make so I feel less overwhelmed?

Give yourself ample time to absorb the crisis and recover.
Has a crisis temporarily knocked you off-balance? Gradually, through routines, periods of solitude and mourning, clarifying priorities, gathering information, support and careful planning, you will feel much more in control.

Impatience is unfair and non-productive. Even though the crisis was sudden, recovery is usually gradual. The time it takes to pull yourself and your life together varies with each individual and circumstance.

How much time do you think it will take you to get re-centered?

When will you again be in charge of your life?

The following chapter discusses the importance of time, how to assess your own readiness and when to make a change.

Chapter 8:
Ready For Action

Getting Ready

People get themselves ready for a change in ways that are not always apparent to anyone else.

I have known Amanda since high school. In the last ten years, I can't recall Amanda saying even once that she would like to get married. Not wanting to give up her freedom or compromise, Amanda had long ago decided that she would remain single.

So I was taken aback when Amanda reversed her position by attending singles socials with an uncharacteristic determination. She spent the better part of a year looking for men. Although Amanda did not date anyone during this time, discouragement never prevented her from continuing what appeared to be a rather fruitless search.

One afternoon when we were idly chatting over a cup of coffee, Amanda mentioned that she had recently met a new male neighbor whom she found quite attractive. They started to date. Within two months, he had moved in. Shortly afterward, they were talking about getting married.

Another friend of mine had a similar experience. Kristen, unlike Amanda, always hoped for marriage. At age 38, Kristen had almost given up hope of ever meeting anyone eligible. The last six months had been especially frustrating. Kristen had met many bachelors, but rapidly discarded them after one evening. Something always seemed to be missing. When a cousin introduced her to a widower named Larry, Kristen was not particularly interested. However, Larry pursued so earnestly that soon Kristen had changed her mind. Four years have passed and they are still happily married.

My shift was clearly self-initiated. For a long time although knowing that my job was no longer appropriate, I never made a serious move. There were several half-hearted attempts at looking for other work. Nothing materialized. No change seemed feasible. I knew that I did not want to stay indefinitely, but I felt stuck. Finally, I decided to take a definite stand. No longer hesitating, I went to my supervisor and handed in a resignation.

Though it may seem as though the three of us altered the course of our lives dramatically with little or no preparation, this was not the case. What was it that precipitated our sudden switching of gears?

It was no coincidence that Amanda and Kristen got married when they did. Both women had made a strong commitment to meeting men. Considerable time and energy had been focused on this goal. Even though the paperwork was executed in one day, I didn't change careers overnight. Two earlier six-month leaves of absence had given me the opportunity to explore other professional worlds and to try on a different lifestyle. Leaving this job was a culmination of extensive soul-searching, dreaming and planning.

Each of us believed that a major change was imperative. The time was right. We were receptive, one-tracked and willing to devote ourselves to the task without any guarantees. Through continuous effort, we created a momentum and laid a foundation for change.

Readiness is a result of many factors. Look at the following diagram to understand the way the keys to change are interrelated:

Getting Ready

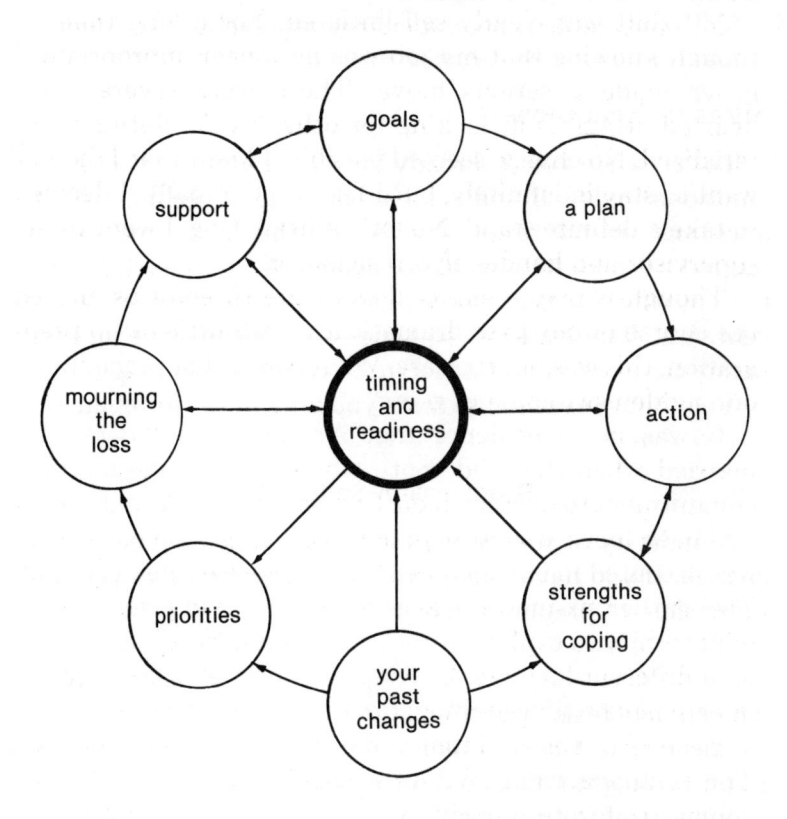

```
            goals
    support      a plan
mourning   timing
the        and      action
loss       readiness
    priorities   strengths
                 for coping
         your
         past
         changes
```

This diagram sums up the previous chapters. Let's review this. To ready yourself for a change, wait until other stresses in your life are at a minimum. Then:

1. Know your pace and follow it as much as possible.
2. Clarify your priorities.
3. Mourn any losses related to this change.
4. Find support so that it is available when you need it.
5. Narrow down your goals so that they are more feasible.
6. Make a plan of action, allowing room for contingency.
7. Get started with small, simple actions.
8. Remind yourself of the changes you made in the past.

Become more aware of your strengths for coping that got you through rough moments.

9. Focus ample time and energy on reaching your goal.

Signs of Readiness

To tell when you feel ready for taking action, check your emotional pulse. If you are panicky, upset, feeling off-balance and overly tense, this is not the best time to get started. Trust that by being aware of your feelings and patient with yourself, you will soon feel stronger and more centered. The passage of time will provide the needed perspective. Soon you'll feel more comfortable.

The following exercise tests your readiness for change.

Readiness: A Self-Test

A majority of *yes* answers indicates your readiness for a change. If you have a majority of *no* answers, give yourself more time to prepare yourself.

	Yes	No
The change feels "right."	___	___
I believe that it can happen.	___	___
I am willing to risk and face the consequences of my actions.	___	___
I expect to devote considerable time and energy toward reaching my goals. I don't expect immediate gratification.	___	___
This change is based upon my own standards, feelings and goals. I am not easily influenced by others.	___	___
I feel reconnected to my past and generally optimistic about the future.	___	___
I can accept sometimes feeling afraid.	___	___
I feel that I have a choice in the matter: either to pursue my goals or to do nothing.	___	___

Should more time be required for your preparation, that

is not unusual. The rhythm of change varies with each individual and cannot be standardized.

The Rhythm of Change

Timing is a highly personal matter. No two people are exactly alike. The pace at which you mature and change is influenced by your upbringing, cumulative experiences, skills, personality, age and environment. Your current financial, professional and marital status also affect the ease with which you take risks.

Just because your best friend married at twenty does not mean that you should. Although there are many people who recover from the death of a spouse in less than two years, four years may be what you need. It is foolish to compare yourself to anyone else or be pressured by how fast you think you should be moving. Your own rhythm takes much less effort and in the long run is more efficient.

The rhythm of change may be:
- slow
- fast
- steady
- uneven
- gradual
- abrupt, in fits and starts

You can expect long periods of rest where nothing seems to be happening. They have value, too. Everyone needs quiet time in which to take a deep breath, evaluate what's been done, and gather energy for the next course of action.

Some people spend weeks mulling over a potential move. Others impulsively jump in with no second thoughts. My own pattern has been rather drastic. I usually have to remove myself from a secure position by cutting all ties. Only when I know I can no longer go back do I feel ready for a change. After wrestling with the idea for a while, I close my eyes, hold my breath and plunge right in. Lorna, a very dear friend, is just the opposite. She is more practical and cautious. Lorna does things more gradually, holding onto security while testing her footing. Jeffrey, another friend, has a different style. He is a systematic, logical planner. Before taking a step, Jeffrey researches as thoroughly as possible, gathering bits of helpful information. This procedure can take anywhere from two weeks to six months.

Think back to the changes you have accomplished in recent years. (You may wish to refresh your memory by referring back to Your Change History Chart.) To familiarize yourself with your habitual style, ask these questions:

- Was I often cautious, impulsive or a planner?
- Did I burn my bridges before making a change, or provide myself with insurance?
- How much did I procrastinate?

Procrastination is a symptom of a lack of readiness. If you put off doing something, like getting a divorce or looking for a better job, assume that it isn't yet the right moment to make a change. So, instead of feeling guilty about what you haven't done, or forcing yourself to act too soon, wait. Later, when you feel more confident or clearer about what you want, you will probably make up for any lost time by accelerating your pace.

Building Momentum

When you feel excited and optimistic, your progress forward is usually amazing. It seems then as though you can do anything. However, such enthusiasm does not last indefinitely. At other moments you may feel exhausted and overwhelmed. Depression and "crashing" from a high are common. To protect yourself, anticipate such swings of mood and try not to be thrown by them.

You build momentum slowly by going forward in small spurts of energy. Each step leads to the next, with the confidence you've acquired helping you to prepare for even more difficult steps.

Momentum is lost when you start to criticize yourself for what you didn't accomplish. This is self-defeating. Don't discount daydreaming about the change. Thinking is a worthwhile activity, as much a source of positive energy as making a phone call, writing a letter, setting up a meeting. Thinking about what you want or intend to do is not enough, but it certainly is a very important beginning.

Instead of being side-tracked or discouraged when nothing seems to be happening right away or when you seem to be going backward, persist. Setbacks are part of the process. Flow with it, and keep your focus on the wider picture. Amanda and Kristen each created a powerful momentum by devoting themselves wholeheartedly to looking for men. Continuous activity does eventually pay off. So relax. The efforts you've made have already set things in motion. Soon you will be able to reap the benefits.

Follow Your Own Timing

You are the only one who knows how much time you actually need to achieve a particular goal. The next exercise clarifies this awareness. I have used it successfully with scores of clients who were amazed at the ease with which they could answer the questions in The Time Test.

The Time Test

State one of your current goals.
Draw a horizontal line, about the width of this page.
Put a small circle at either end of this line.

•————————————————————————————•

The left-hand circle represents the moment you first established this as a goal. The right-hand mark signifies when you will reach it.

Think for a minute. How much have you already accomplished toward this end? Put a third mark somewhere in-between the two circles to symbolize where you are today in terms of your goal.

Now consider how long it took you to reach the second

mark, and how much more time you think is necessary to reach the third mark.

Follow the same procedure for several additional goals, drawing a separate line for each one.

•───────────────────────────────•

Goal 2:

•───────────────────────────────•

Goal 3:

•───────────────────────────────•

Goal 4:

Be sure to include your present position in the line reference to each goal, by placing a third circle on each line in-between the other two.

Then, on the following chart, enter your four goals in the first column. Fill in the information requested in the second column, using your best estimate.

Goals	Time Allotted (estimate)
1.	
2.	
3.	
4.	

Because of impatience, you may push yourself to accomplish too much too soon. To avoid this snag, ask:
- Am I being realistic in the time I have given myself?
- Would it be more practical to lengthen (or shorten) it?

Follow your inner clock rather than selecting th time you think you *should* be finished. Don't compare yourself to others or to some impossible standard of perfection. The object is for you to feel as comfortable as possible, unpressured, with enough breathing space and room for contingency. There is enough stress in most change without your adding more. Trust that with intuition and careful probing you have a very good sense of how much time is needed.

Add a third column to the chart, modifying the time you have allotted as you see fit:

Goals	Time Allotted (estimate)	Modified Time
1.		
2.		
3.		
4.		

Planning

A goal gives purpose and direction to your life, making it seem less humdrum, helping you to feel more in charge. Planning supplies a systematic and practical way of getting you to a destination.

Although a plan consists of several consecutive steps to take, you needn't feel compelled to follow it to the letter. It is merely a map, an outline of activities within a time framework. Flexibility is imperative. Try to be open enough to adapt to new situations, seize new opportunities or discard a plan.

You'll need a tentative plan for reaching each goal. The goal should be small enough so that you can accomplish it within a short time.

Head a fresh page, "Planning For Change." Put today's date at the top. Under it, list one current goal. Leave room for possible actions to take.

Planning For Change

Date:
Goal #1: Actions	Suggested Date	When Accomplished
1.		
2.		
3.		
4.		
5.		

Be sure to start with things you find easy to execute. Trying to tackle huge tasks is overwhelming. For example, if you are cleaning up clutter in your home, attack only one room or one corner of a room at a time rather than trying to restore the entire house at once. Use verbs in short phrases to describe possible actions. Here is a sample chart started for the goal: "To live within my income of $200/week":

Actions	Suggested Date	When Accomplished
1. Make the commitment to spend less money than I make.	Monday	
2. List those items that are absolutely necessary (food, rent, telephone, electricity, transportation).	Monday	
3. Write down what I actually spend each day.	Monday–Sunday	
4. Check those items that add pleasure but which I don't actually need.	Tuesday	
5. Omit at least 3 items and substitute others that are either free or cost less.	Tuesday	
6. Make a preliminary budget	Tuesday	
7. Look at my feelings about spending money.	Daily	
8. Allow myself one day this week to be extravagant, but do not spend more than $20.	Saturday	
9. Talk to my friends about how they budget.	Wednesday	
10.		
11.		
12.		

Add the last three actions yourself.

You may include whimsical, creative, funny things to do that are not directly on target. The idea is to generate energy through activity, without your closing any doors by being too practical or restrictive. For example, to continue the list of actions for the goal, "To live within my income of $200/week," you may write:
- Go windowshopping without buying anything.

- Fantasize myself very rich.
- Imagine myself flat broke.

Besides the immediate steps which you can take today or this week, also consider what you can do in the next month or two. Keep your list of accomplishments up to date and reward yourself accordingly. Add any items that are not on your planning list that you may spontaneously do.

Finding Support When You Need It

Support is crucial at every stage of making a change. It helps you to overcome fear, mourn any losses, fantasize success, clarify priorities, set goals, plan, follow your own timing, get ready faster and take action:

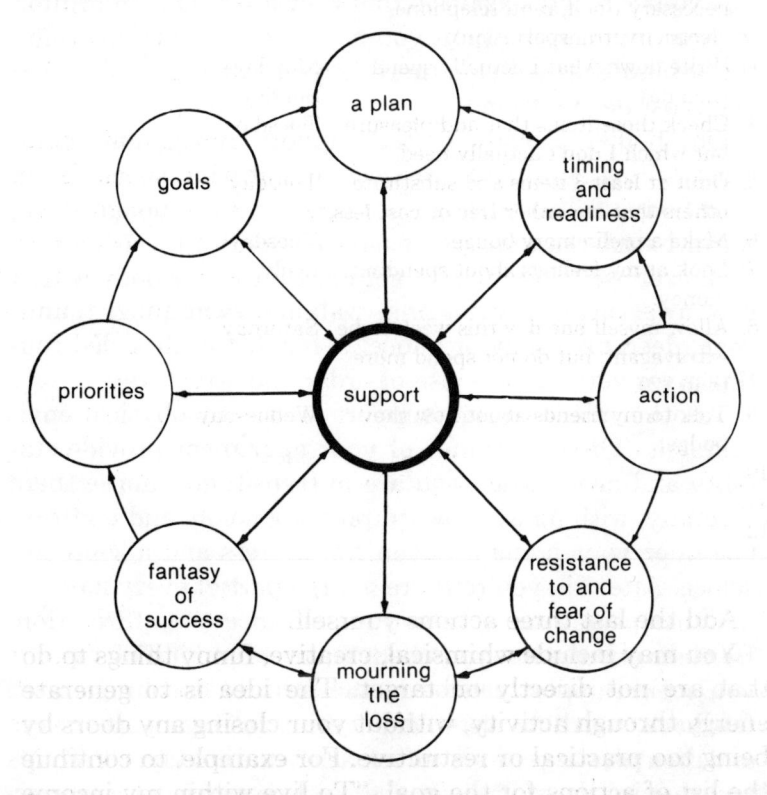

When Support Is Helpful

Since changing can be lonely and scary in the beginning, having a ready-made support system is important. Those close to you may feel threatened by the risks you are taking for a while, so you'll need to look in other places for support.

A person to turn to for support may be someone you haven't thought of—yourself. Be there emotionally for yourself by pampering yourself often. This is not self-indulgence at all. Give yourself praise instead of a hard time for what you haven't yet accomplished. If you've been actively pursuing your goals, take a short rest in order to recover your enthusiasm and energy. During rough times, be your friend, not your enemy.

Focus on all the positive things you have done. Remember how successfully you have coped in other situations. List your strengths again so that they are freshly imprinted in your mind. Rely upon yourself in a new way. Develop the habit of always being there for yourself, especially when you most need a friend.

Our bodies provide special support by signaling emotions, telling us when to proceed and at what speed. Keep your body healthy through proper nutrition, enough sleep, warm baths, massage and exercise. Besides releasing tension, exercise allows you to get back into your body with a new awareness. Try jogging, walking, swimming, tennis, yoga, deep breathing or dance. A regularly scheduled routine gives your day a sense of order and structure.

Another place to find support is in your physical environment. The furnishings of your apartment provide stability and peace when you are in transition. Choose them carefully, with an eye toward pleasing colors and textures. Consider your home a haven from stress and a source of solace. After all, you're there a large part of every day.

Other people can give you reassurance and affirmation. Be clear about what you need, about what kind of support you seek. Support can be in the form of encouragement, feedback, touching, listening, sharing feelings, experiences and dreams, suggestions, information and contacts. Perhaps you require the skilled services and resources of a lawyer, accountant, housekeeper, babysitter, therapist or literary agent.

If you are in transition, it's great to be near people who encourage change, boost your ego, provide continuity and a sense of community. Lasting friendships give you the feeling that your world is stable. When you are feeling a little shaky, it is very reassuring to be able to lean on someone else. Brief encounters are also gratifying. I have had delightful conversations of surprising depth and realness, received helpful suggestions and begun potentially rewarding relationships by being receptive to relative strangers. Tenant meetings, workshops, professional associations and even ticket lines open up all kinds of possibilities for momentary support and add new people to your life.

Look at the quality of your current relationships and at the degree of intimacy and nurturing they supply. Who supports your growth? With whom do you share your dreams?

When your morale is low, it's best to discuss your plans only with those whose attitude is supportive. They will help you to clarify your true feelings and try out your wings.

Instead of assuming that they can read your mind, reach out to others when you're feeling needy. Try to become more aware of the way you communicate and if it generally elicits a positive response. Demanding something because you feel desperate puts too much pressure on people and therefore usually produces reactions of anger or guilt. It would be more effective to give others a choice of whether or not to get involved. For example, you might say, "I'm feeling shaky today. I value your friendship and would appreciate spending some time with you this afternoon, for about an hour or so. If this is not convenient, perhaps we can arrange something later in the week. Just looking forward to being together will help me to get through the day and cheer me up immensely." Be as specific as possible about what you would like your friend to do: go with you to a movie, listen quietly, offer advice or reassurance.

Live in the moment, trusting that tomorrow will take care of itself. Cherish unexpected meetings and small gestures of warmth. Bryna, my wise friend, once gave me some advice that you may find as practical as I did for the times when you are feeling blue. Her suggestion was to bank any happy moments. Later, when you're less secure, these pleasant memories can be used to lighten what had started out as a very discouraging day.

Plotting Your Progress

Regardless of how you felt when you started reading this book, assume that your interest and efforts will lead to success. Trust the process and your ability to synthesize what you don't yet know consciously. Feel confident about handling all the practical details it takes to create a new and satisfying lifestyle. You've acquired the tools to effectively evaluate your current needs and priorities, eliminate most obstacles, shift direction and generate action. These tools provide additional support for change.

It's wise to set up a regular space in your busy week for working on change. So that it becomes a habit, schedule blocks of time during every week for this purpose. During these sessions look at the diagrams in the beginning of the book, read the notes you have written, think about what you've already accomplished, update your priorities and goals, revise your plans, identify new fears and resistance to change that come up as you take action, review the exercises (especially the ones where you need more work), and compare today's results with your earlier efforts. It is foolish and counterproductive to chastise yourself for how little you have done. Please remember that *thinking* about what has happened and where you are going is a valuable activity which clarifies feelings and direction so that action is possible.

It helps to realize that this is an *ongoing* process which does not necessarily occur at a steady pace. Compare your rhythm of change now with what it was when you first started reading this book. Make certain that your list of actions (however small they may be) is up-to-date. Keep track of what you do and when you do it to see if there are any patterns in your activity.

If you perceive that you are alone too much, devote some energy to expanding your support network. Use the time you have set aside for working on change to call friends and schedule appointments with them.

Be flexible in the way you proceed. If you miss a day because you are otherwise occupied, it is not a catastrophe. What counts is not a rigid schedule, but your degree of commitment. Here is a typical third week of changemaking.

Sunday.

Evening: Give myself credit for what I've accomplished so far. Review Gold Stars exercise.

Review The Time Test.

Monday.

Morning: Physical exercise to release tension.

Look at last week's goals and check which ones were not yet accomplished. Decide what information or resources I need and how to obtain them. Set new goals and plan actions for this week.

Review Skyhooks exercise in reference to these goals.

Review Mourning exercise in reference to these goals.

Tuesday.

Morning through afternoon: Remind myself of my strengths. Review Your Reserve Bank exercise.

Make calls, set up appointments, do research or carry out two planned actions relevant to my week's goals.

Wednesday.

Morning: Continue planned actions.

All day: Identify any new fears that arise. Review Dark Clouds and Red Flags exercises.

Evening: Physical exercise.

Thursday.

Relaxation. Devote today to pleasure, to a vacation from actively working on change. Try not to take anything seriously.

Friday.

Evening: Have Jane and Bob, who are also making

changes in their lives, over for dinner. Discuss what we have accomplished so far this week. Share our dreams of the future and feelings of fear. Establish a regular support system.

Saturday.
    Morning: Physical exercise.
    Review Worry Beads exercise.

Sunday.
    Evening: Review Piecework exercise.
    Decide what kind of support I need or want this week, and where to obtain it.

Support is both your lifeline and an impetus for change. Finding it adds the final link in a chain of resources and strategies. It is time to apply them toward actualizing your dreams.

Part Four: Focus

Chapter 9: Coping with Unemployment

Why We Work

Why do you work?

The answer is fairly obvious: to make a living. There are endless bills to be paid, including rent, groceries, utilities, transportation, telephone, insurance, doctors and entertainment. But money is not the only incentive. Besides providing necessary income, work serves several other purposes. Reporting to a job on a daily basis gives you a sense of belonging and the opportunity to be with others and to feel useful. The continuity and structure of a familiar environment and customary routines add to your inner security and well-being.

The Benefits of Working

If you are working now, use your present job as a point of reference. If you're not employed, think about the rewards of previous or possible future jobs. Which of the following are your reasons?

- status   ____
- recognition   ____
- power   ____
- responsibility   ____
- contact with people ____
- challenge   ____
- a place to go every day ____

- a feeling of usefulness
- a sense of personal impact
- structure
- money
- pleasure
- self-fulfillment and inner satisfaction
- a sense of identity and belonging
- utilization of your talents and skills
- a direction and purpose in life

Add any other benefits that are important to you.

Being Jobless

With all of these benefits, working provides the framework for a meaningful lifestyle. In a work-oriented society, most people have some kind of a job. Anyone who is unemployed probably feels like a member of an unpopular minority. Because roles have changed and the economy is unpredictable, many women with children and people who don't actually need a salary are part of the work force.

You will probably experience several periods of unemployment during your working life. Your reactions may be relief, excitement, a sense of adventure, fear, self-doubt, a sense of unfairness, shame or confusion about what to do next. How you respond depends largely upon why you are unemployed, whose decision it was, your age, financial status and how long the period of time involved.

Unemployment is sometimes involuntary. When your position is terminated, your are fired, the company goes bankrupt or relocates with only a fraction of the staff, someone else is calling the shots. The lack of income, enforced leisure and uncertainty about how long you'll be out of work will cause additional stress.

Determining *when* to leave your job makes you feel in control of your life. Having a choice in the matter makes you feel more autonomous.

If you are unexpectedly out of work at age 50, you'll

probably feel anxious. Time seems to pass at a snail's pace when you don't have anything important to do. A tight job market, inflation, the high cost of living and piled up bills can be rather discouraging. However, try not to discount the many years you were working, the skills, experiences and knowledge acquired that make you highly employable. Your financial assets (a savings account, bonds, the equity of a house or land) can be very reassuring during extended periods of unemployment. It's always a good idea to bank enough funds to last for a three to six month emergency. This cushion alleviates a degree of stress.

Negative thinking about a situation only makes it worse. We will explore ways to change your attitude, so that you're better equipped to handle the time between jobs.

Unemployment and Self-Fulfilling Prophecies

When you are unemployed, your major preoccupations are usually money, getting another job and making the period with no income as brief as possible. Such a focus puts you in an underdog position. Overly aware of what you don't have, you are operating from deficiency instead of from strength. Such an attitude can keep you unemployed longer, since it sets up self-fulfilling prophecies.

There are basically three kinds of negative thinking that are relevant here.

- A negative attitude toward money
- A fear of rejection
- A lack of perspective about time

We'll explore each of them individually.

A negative attitude toward money.

Eloise frets constantly about money. An English major, Eloise's first position was as an editorial assistant. Because Eloise felt unchallenged, she quit and took a job as manager of a pet store. After three months, by mutual agreement, Eloise left. Five months of unemployment ensued. Even though it was self-initiated, Eloise found this period very difficult.

"I was very worried. With no savings, it was really hand-to-mouth. I watched every single penny and felt anxious all the time. When people asked me what I was doing, I felt ashamed. My self-esteem was so low that I would do anything for a few bucks."

Focused only on surviving, Eloise probably set her sights too low. She was on a perpetual economic treadmill.

A negative attitude about money can put you in the same position as Eloise, regardless of how much money you actually have. Are you anxious about money, doubtful of your earning powers? Do you despair about never having enough money to live comfortably? If so, try to remember that confronting a negative attitude is the first step in developing a positive one.

A fear of rejection keeps you from looking for work with confidence.

Unless your sense of self is very strong, job rejections reinforce another destructive self-fulfilling prophecy. Thinking, "I'm not valuable enough to be hired," you blame the present situation on your lack of worth. Your self-defeating attitude influences the way you present yourself to prospective employers.

This was what happened to Charlotte, an aspiring actress. Charlotte was only twenty-six when she spent a year looking for work in the theater after a four-year stint as a clerk-typist.

"I went to auditions, but soon started losing my confidence. The idea of being rejected was so frightening that I went through a period after each audition when I couldn't talk to anyone for three or four days. My feelings of personal inadequacy got worse. Depression started affecting everything else." Charlotte lacked a positive self-image. Her identity was too dependent upon other people's approval. Unemployment only clarified Charlotte's insecurities. In order to continue in her career, Charlotte had to develop more confidence and a much thicker skin.

If your identity is too closely connected with your job,

you might work on separating who you are from what you do.

A lack of perspective about time makes this moment seem as though it will last forever. You assume that you will always be unemployed.

Inactivity is a problem. When most days are relatively unstructured, it's difficult to find the incentive to get up in the morning or utilize free time constructively.

Unemployment thrusts you into long stretches of time alone. If you don't enjoy your own company or know how to organize the hours for productive and pleasurable activity, this is a splendid opportunity to learn.

The secret to getting ahead in life is to use whatever situation you find yourself in as a means of increasing your self-knowledge and coping skills.

Once you become aware of them, any self-fulfilling prophecies you may be holding onto will no longer rule your life. The trend can easily be reversed.

Reversing the Trend

Unemployment does not have to be unpleasant or depressing. To many people it is a time for introspection. They can think more clearly about the kind of work they will do and the lifestyle they want. Freed from a nine-to-five routine, there is space to dream and to strengthen inner resources.

For Eloise and Charlotte, unemployment was a prelude to a career change. Eloise eventually became a communications consultant. The months out of work gave Eloise the time to assess her skills, values, weaknesses and direction. She decided that there was no longer to be any limit on her earning capacity. At thirty-four, after only a few years, her career is flourishing. Charlotte realized that the perfect theater job would have to wait. She needed a skill in order to pay the bills until she became more established as an actress. Word processing school provided a practical answer. It also took the pressure off her desperation to get a part when she went to auditions. Rejections became less important to Charlotte when the rent was paid by temporary but high-paying jobs between her roles.

To cope with unemployment, you must reverse the trend of self-fulfilling prophecies. After catching yourself in the act, break the vicious circle by more positive thinking.

Develop a more positive attitude about money and your earning capacity.

If you focus on merely surviving, you'll find it difficult to achieve more than this. Most of your energy will go into the struggle to make ends meet. With this attitude, unemployment means hard times economically. In fact, this lack of faith actually prevents your circumstances from changing.

A positive attitude toward money helps you to view life from a position of abundance rather than deprivation. Being without funds is then only temporary. You're sure about your abilities and future success. If today looks bleak, tomorrow will be better. Unemployment is a period of transition, a time to generate new ideas which will bring financial reward in the future.

Although it's hard not to worry about money, you can pull yourself out of such negative thinking by applying The Fantasy of Success.

During the times when there are no definite job offers in sight, imagine that you are being offered three very attractive positions. Then visualize yourself making a choice. Fantasize yourself enjoying your work and receiving a high salary. Fill in the details concerning your actual responsibilities, surroundings and typical working day.

Decide how much money you would *like* to make, even if this seems to be unrealistic. Picture yourself getting a check much larger than your usual weekly salary, and happily spending every penny—with no guilt. Make the amount large enough to cover all your current expenses with a considerable amount left over for fun. In what way would you spend money for pleasure?

Repeat these fantasies until you start to believe that you are deserving enough so that these pie-in-the-sky dreams could come true. The purpose of doing this is to get you out of the hole of despair by swinging first to the upbeat extreme. Then, after trying such a playful outlook on for size, measure your dreams against reality and adjust them. Eventually such continuous optimistic refocusing will reverse your luck.

To avoid being crushed by a series of rejections, begin to develop a strong sense of self.

First separate yourself from your work. Your work is not "you." If you can do this successfully, you will find that your attitude frees you to perform on a higher level.

Instill faith in yourself by saying the following aloud every day, at least twice a day:

"I know that I will soon find a job that suits me."

Stop convincing yourself that if it doesn't happen immediately, this is proof that there is something very much wrong with you. To reinforce a positive attitude, add:

"I am a worthwhile person even if I am not immediately hired."

Be sure that you don't expect everyone to automatically know your abilities. Present yourself with your best foot forward by summarizing your assets, not apologizing for being without a job. Know what you have to offer to potential employers. Eloise and Charlotte spent many hours assessing their skills. This gave them much more confidence in facing job interviews.

What are your special qualifications? In what do you excel? Here, again, concentrate on what you did well at your last job, rather than upon your failures. If you lack skill, think about where you can quickly learn what is lacking and acquire it.

Keep your perspective by taking only one day at a time.
Realize that this period of unemployment is only temporary.

Plan each day very carefully, as though it were important. Treasure the time that you have and use it lovingly.

Provide regularity through daily routines done at the same time: exercise, walking the dog, making business calls, keeping up with correspondence, buying a newspaper and reading it. You might also set the clock to waken you exactly as if you had to travel to work. These routines give you a sense of order and continuity at a time when they are generally lacking.

Exercise releases tension and stimulates your respiratory system. As a result you feel more lively and enthusiastic. My eight a.m. tennis game begins my morning schedule seven months a year and provides the continuity that freelancing cannot. In the cooler weather, when the courts are closed, I swim at a local health club. On the days that I don't exercise, I am irritable or fidgety.

Treat the morning hours as the start of a normal working day. List at least three things you want to accomplish by tomorrow. Establish goals that are readily achieved. Then take credit for your efforts (see Gold Stars).

Give yourself enough options so that you don't feel trapped. Will you make a phone call or write a letter to that new contact? If someone you want to see is busy, try to see them later in the week—or even next week. This flexibility gives you the space to breathe. It also keeps you open to spontaneity so that you can flow with whatever happens, seizing every possible opportunity.

Add the ingredient of pleasure so that you are concentrating upon more than finding a job. See a friend, go for a stroll, splurge on a movie or concert, even if you are short of cash. Treating yourself like a V.I.P. enables you to project a more positive image.

Take pride in your appearance, even when you have no appointments scheduled. Convince yourself that you are just as important and your life as meaningful as when you were working.

Think about what you can do to lessen any stress you may feel.

Take especially good care of your body to avoid becoming ill or rundown. Eliminate any unnecessary pressure by remembering that this period is not going to last forever. You will get a job. Meanwhile, give yourself whatever support you lack by treating yourself with extra gentleness.

Build a network by telling everyone you know that you are looking for work, and ask them for names of people to see. Spend time with people whom you know from past experience will be encouraging. The last thing you need now is criticism for not finding a new job soon enough.

Plan social engagements at least three times a week to give you some balance. Looking for a job is hard work!

If you have sufficient funds to last six months, try not to panic when you've been unemployed for only one month. Without enough cash to cover your expenses, it would be to your advantage to find temporary work until you find more suitable employment.

Positive Rethinking

The key points to remember when you are facing unemployment are:

- Clarify your reasons for working.
- Understand why you are not working now.
- Confront all your feelings about looking for work and being unemployed.
- Go over your financial situation: get a clear picture of your assets and liabilities.
- Decide how much money you a) actually need and b) want—and why.
- Develop a more positive attitude about money.
- Concentrate on your strengths by assessing your skills.
- Separate yourself from your work so that you can accept rejections if they come.
- Fantasize yourself working and being successful.
- Live in the moment with a plan for the future.
- Establish routines to organize your day.
- Take care of your body.
- Find support: from activities, other people and yourself.

By changing your attitude and behavior, you will make unemployment a satisfying and productive part of your life that you will be proud to recall.

Chapter 10: Career Transitions

Your Changing Work Status

- "Great news dear: I've just been promoted!"
- "Now that the children are older, I can go back to work."
- "My company is moving out of state, but I am not prepared to go. So I will have to find another job."
- "I'm bored with this job."
- "They made me an offer I can't resist, so I've given two weeks notice."
- "My new boss and I don't see eye to eye. I'm thinking of transferring to another department."
- "There's no room for advancement here. It's time for a change."

For any number of reasons like these, people frequently leave their jobs. If you are presently or soon to be employed, you can expect to shift several times in your career.

Transitions in work occur at all stages of your working life. Sometimes they are directed toward moving up the ladder of success. More lucrative or challenging positions are sought by those who want to improve their lot. Perhaps after years spent performing in one professional area, you will look for ways to try your hand at something else. This may mean changing your field. If you are a parent who devoted many years to raising a family, being paid for your work is an important change. In your later years, the possibility of retirement opens new vistas, especially when you are not lacking in capital.

A New Work Ethic Makes Career Change More Likely

Can you envision a career change in the foreseeable future?

Regardless of your age, qualifications or present job status, a career change may lie ahead. The occupation you selected many years ago is not necessarily the one that you will follow forever. Are you a paper hanger but yearn for the stage? Are you tired of driving a taxicab or teaching school? You can make your dreams a reality by shifting to another field.

At this very minute, millions of adults are quite seriously considering changing their professions. People used to be trained for one kind of work that lasted a lifetime. But the modern world has different pressures and options. Technology separates many workers from the fruits of their labor. Their sense of accomplishment is diminished. Jobs are often so specialized that after only five or ten years, 'burnout' sets in. Economic factors, less stereotyped sex roles and new attitudes toward working have made career change a feasible and healthy alternative.

Economic factors. Recession and a shrinking job market have compelled those who earn their living to think in more practical terms. Frightened of losing a main source of income through cutbacks or layoffs, the more practical individual plans ahead for such an eventuality. Just in case it is ever called for, the foundation for a new occupation is already set.

New sex roles. No longer is the man in the family its sole breadwinner. Wives share the burden of bringing home enough money so that the couple can afford a comfortable standard of living even in inflation and hard times. Single women who are self-supporting have also realized the value of a career instead of a job.

Attitudes toward work. Since so many hours of the week are spent by so many people at work, job satisfaction has become as important as their monetary reward. A recent emphasis on the quality of work life influences people to reevaluate the kind of work that they perform. Those willing to risk a change, college students with foresight in a tight job market, mothers ready to return to the work force, middle-aged executives seeking new options and adventurous retirees are all shifting their focus. They may go back to college for a degree in a different field, start a business, develop a favorite hobby for income or explore as yet untapped skills. People are preparing themselves for the future, wanting to have more choices about what work to do and where to do it.

When You Want To Leave Your Job

If you are seriously thinking about a second career, how can you get started?

Before taking the plunge, I suggest that you first weigh several issues. To organize your thinking, answer the following questions. You might also discuss your feelings with a sympathetic friend who is usually objective.

Why do you want to change your occupation? What is wrong with your current job?

Look closely at your present situation. Try to analyze the cause of your dissatisfaction. Do you enjoy the physical environment in which you work? Or are you bored with being in the same place for many years? Rather than a career change, what you need may be a new firm with different surroundings!

Relationships with people can be a major stumbling block causing job dissatisfaction. Examine and take the responsibility for your own part in how you are treated by co-workers and your boss. Are you assertive or do you usually overreact? Think about what you can do to improve your communication and eliminate negative interaction. You certainly would not want to switch jobs and then discover that the same problems have followed you. First see if you can resolve the situation. If it then seems that the problem is insurmountable, go elsewhere. However, this doesn't necessarily mean moving to a different field.

Next, look at the kind of work you are now performing.

In what ways is it satisfying? What is missing that you need? Be clear about your motivation for leaving your present field. Common reasons for wanting a second career are more challenge, money, power, responsibilty, variety or flexible hours. To further clarify your motivation review the exercises Skyhooks, Priorities and The Benefits of Working.

Why haven't you made this change before?

Several female clients told me that they didn't want to change careers before their children were of school age. In order to be at home for a large part of the day, they were presently working part-time or at jobs with flexible hours. Others said that it had taken them until now to properly assess their transferrable skills or build enough confidence to risk the change. Additional reasons for waiting were a lack of funds, incomplete training or not knowing what they wanted to do.

People also delay when their motivation is not sufficiently high or when their goals are unfocused. Gregory, a writer, did not change his career until he felt pushed against the wall. A former vice president who sacrificed a very lucrative position, Gregory explained his evolution. "I spent my entire life being what I thought other people wanted me to be. My goals really had nothing to do with who I was. I very much wanted to write. It became increasingly painful not to be where I wanted to be professionally. My frustration mounted until I knew that I had to find a way to get out. That's when I quit."

What are you most fearful of or anxious about in making this change?

One of the chief worries of many people is being too old to be considered for a substantial position. The reality of the situation is that discrimination because of age, even though against the law, sometimes does exist. Nevertheless, you needn't let this stop you from feeling optimistic. There are numerous success stories of older men and women who were determined to get ahead.

• My friend and colleague, Ruth, was forty-seven when she gave up being an advertising and public relations writer to do career counseling. When we first met, although Ruth had been in practice only for a short time, her reputation was already widespread.

• At fifty-five, Lois closed a family business and three months later was managing a lecture bureau.

•Alice was forty-six when she left computer programming to be a technical writer in the health field.

• When Gregory was forty-four, even though he was fairly well established in the business world, he devoted himself to writing on a full-time basis. Since then Gregory has had several books and articles published and is happily ensconced in a new career.

There are countless others who received recognition in a second field and surpass their original incomes. What it takes is fortitude, confidence, patience and a willingness to risk. Age may make you hesitate, but it does not have to prevent you from building a dream.

What frightens you about leaving your present line of work? Typical worries about a career change are not being hired, being out of work forever, not making enough money, being fired for incompetence, feeling out of control of your life, being unable to compete with others for a position, feeling stupid or inadequate, not liking the new field any better than the previous one and the passage of time.

Make a list of your own fears. Remember that being able to articulate your fears will help you to overcome them.

How long do you think it will take you to establish yourself in a new career?

If you expect to find the perfect job tomorrow, you are unnecessarily adding pressure to an already stressful search. Treat each new position you accept as a bridge to the next. One job may increase your confidence, another teach you new skills, a third give you added responsibility or experience. Your reputation and professional worth come from expertise acquired gradually, over time. No career change is accomplished in one step. Assume that if you desire a higher salary or position it may take longer than if you were less selective.

With this in mind, try to give yourself at least three

months to land that first job in a new field. Add time for possible family emergencies, a lagging economy, illness, procrastination or changing your mind about the kind of position you're seeking.

What have you already accomplished toward changing your career?

Assume that you've already started the process. You've devoted considerable thought to the possibility of a change. You're reading this book. You've probably spoken to many people about their work and consulted your address book for additional contacts.

Now consider what you can do this coming week that is related to your goal. It may be writing a resume, making a call to set up an appointment, doing research on possible fields, thinking about your priorities, interests and aptitudes, discussing your plans and fears with a friend, buying a job-hunting wardrobe or being interviewed for a job. Whatever you actually do, be sure to pat yourself on the back for your efforts.

Many career-changers are so busy focusing on their future success that they fail to notice how far along they have already travelled and give up in discouragement.

Issues To Consider

One question many career changers ask is *"Should I get further education to better prepare myself for a new field?"* You can decide this by looking at the quality of available training and the consequences of proceeding without it. Speak to people in the field you are investigating about their own qualifications. Perhaps they know of practical shortcuts.

There are two opposing views on this issue. On the negative side, going back to school is seen as a means of avoiding the job-hunting jungle because it removes you, at least temporarily, from the work world. Training places you in a relatively cloistered and safe environment and can prolong the preparatory period for several years. On the other hand, the benefits are numerous. An education facilitates your learning the vocabulary of a new field, gives you an excellent theoretical foundation and an overview of the kinds of jobs presently available.

Although additional courses can add to your credibility and confidence, they aren't imperative. Formal education is not a substitute for first-hand experience. To make a decision, consider whether further training will increase your confidence so that you can present yourself most positively to others in your new field. Find out what qualifications are considered mandatory. Between what you would like to learn and what you are expected to learn, some courses may be necessary.

Another problem common to career changers is procrastination. Suppose that after making the decision and beginning exploratory research into possible career fields, your initial surge of enthusiasm wanes. Weeks slip by, yet your progress is miniscule or nonexistent. Your feet feel as though they are glued to one spot. You cannot move. Your frustration increases because it seems as though you will never be able to get out of this morass.

If this actually happens, what can you do?

First, I suggest that you accept your own need to procrastinate. You have to drag your feet for a while. This doesn't mean that you'll never be ready to do anything. Trust that eventually you'll move ahead. Next, even though you would much rather do nothing right now, stretch yourself a little farther by attempting some simple task related to your career. Your focus should be on getting started, on putting yourself in motion. Then congratulate yourself for your efforts rather than on what was actually accomplished.

Thirdly, verify that your procrastination is not the result of fears that you've been ignoring. You might want to look further into the origin of your hesitation by reviewing the exercise Dark Clouds in Chapter 3.

Prime yourself for action by going over the material on timing and readiness in Chapter 8, especially the exercises Readiness: A Self-Test and The Time Test.

Lastly, look at what was accomplished so far and compare it to what still remains to be done. Give yourself ample time with room for contingency, setbacks or rethinking your direction.

The Older Person's Predicament

When you have survived a lifetime of employment and put job and career changes behind, you may be ready for still another work transition. After working hard for so many years, retirement may seem like a blessing. Consistent efforts and diligence are to be rewarded. Now you are finally going to relax and enjoy life. How will you occupy your time when you have the luxury of unlimited hours in which to do exactly what you please? Some senior citizens are engrossed in meaningful volunteer work. Others spend time with grandchildren, travel, talk to good friends, garden, play tennis, read, catch up on long-forgotten hobbies like painting or sewing or carpentry.

For people who are financially secure, emotionally stable, physically healthy, socially adept and mentally aware, retirement will pose few problems. Family ties and a multitude of interests provide them with enumerable alternatives. However, for others the picture is not always so rosy because retirement creates anxiety and stress.

Sarah retired three years ago when she was sixty-six. Even though she was married and quite comfortable financially, Sarah felt restless and dissatisfied. "At first I was afraid of getting up in the morning with nothing to do. I felt that I had lost my independence. What I missed most was the relationships, feedback, having a professional identity and getting intellectual stimulation. Instead of feeling productive, creative and needed, I felt frustrated and disappointed.

"The first few months were the hardest because I still didn't know what I needed or wanted. So I kept busy, jumping from one thing to another, taking whatever came along. I couldn't even say no because then I would have had nothing to do. Without my public relations job I either procrastinated or filled my calendar with meetings and social engagements so as not to be bored. Although I had no time to think, I managed to feel cheated."

Sarah's sense of isolation was exacerbated by the fact that her two sons, of whom she was very fond, lived at a considerable distance. Frustrated by friendships she had outgrown, Sarah felt entirely too dependent upon her husband.

Jennifer, unlike Sarah, did not voluntarily retire. Budgetary cuts eradicated Jennifer's professorial position in a large university. Subsequently, Jennifer felt as isolated as Sarah. Her husband was still working and both daughters were married and lived out of state. She saw their one grandchild only a few times a year.

Jennifer is vibrant, slim and looks much younger than her fifty-nine years. With great intensity of feeling, she recalls, "When the crunch came, there were rumors. However, I never really thought that I would be affected. When I cleaned out my desk and returned my keys, it hurt. To me it seemed that everything that mattered was being taken away. I have so much to contribute and love teaching. It was so terribly unfair. Because my husband was heavily in debt, I was anxious about money. Our car had been repossessed and I was afraid we would soon lose our house. It was a bad financial scene.

"Physically, it was as though I was hollow inside. My gums, teeth and ears ached and I was often dizzy. My job was always a major part of my identity. Now I felt disconnected, aimless, wasted, fearful of the future, off-balance, overly dependent, inferior and unmotivated to do anything about my situation.

"Losing my job meant that I was only a mother and wife. I have to be my own person. I never expected or wanted to retire. Everyone else was busy and involved. I felt trapped and forgotten by the world. I didn't want to spend the rest of my life shopping in department stores and eating in restaurants. I was still young enough to work."

Ramon's reactions to unstructured time were quite similar to Sarah's and Jennifer's. A year ago, when he was sixty-five, Ramon retired from a career in sales. Although the decision was his, Ramon did not find things as easy as he had anticipated.

"The stress at my job was so great for the last two years that I certainly wanted to leave. I knew that social security would ease any financial burden and that I had enough interests with which to occupy myself. But I was still concerned about money. I've always been extremely active and busy. I never could sit still, even for a minute. Now I had nothing definite to do. I felt as though I were turning into a lump of lard. I had no real direction, only a vague idea of what I wanted to do with my free time. What I thought about was conducting seminars and sales meetings for industrial corporations, yet I had no degree or experience. So I felt very insecure and inadequate, depressed and doubtful of my chances."

Sarah, Jennifer and Ramon express feelings typical of new retirees. Are any of the following reactions yours?

Common Feelings About Retirement
- a sense of worthlessness
- loneliness and isolation
- an inability to structure time
- a loss of identity and prestige
- feeling 'put out to pasture'
- an obsession with getting older or dying
- anxiety about money

Overcoming The Blues

It is possible to overcome these problems and regain your equilibrium. Each of the three retirees explained how this was accomplished.

Sarah learned that she needed time to carefully sort things out. "I am somewhat indecisive. It took me three years to leave and another three to get used to not working. By stumbling through things I didn't like in order to find out what I did want to do, I gradually developed more confidence. This helped me to set new priorities. I understand how important it is for me to be in the limelight. I am much stronger now and find it easier to be alone than

I would have thought. I am able to make choices without being so easily influenced and can say no with far greater assurance." Sarah is busy with meetings and social functions of several religious and cultural organizations. She also presents lectures on popular topics. These activities give Sarah satisfaction. Her friendships have deepened with the people who share similar interests. In the evenings Sarah and her husband entertain, go to the theater or relax.

Jennifer coped in a different way with her transition. "I did a lot of crying, especially for my husband. Of the two of us, I had previously been the strong one." Then she started to make lists, filling pages with tempting things to do. Jennifer is a painter. One of the items on her list was to exhibit her work more frequently. She began to prepare for several upcoming shows. Another idea was to accompany her husband on short business trips.

After a few months, just as Jennifer was beginning to accept this new unstructured lifestyle, she was offered a part-time position at the university. Even though the salary was considerably lower than before, Jennifer accepted gratefully. "When I am working, I feel focused, fulfilled, appreciated, awake, healthy, centered and independent. Since I get my kicks from relating to people, I come home feeling very high. Aren't I lucky to be able to earn a living this way?"

With persistence, Ramon conquered his depressions and is well on the way to a satisfying second career. Like Jennifer, Ramon is happiest when he is working. Ramon speaks about his experiences with great pride in his voice. "What kept me going was the fantasy that something would turn up tomorrow. I always had this strong feeling that something would happen soon. And it did, slowly but surely. I started my first adult education course before I left my job. That's when I discovered that I loved teaching and was good at it. My evaluations were glowing.

"To get more jobs, I spent a lot of time visiting school districts, deans and coordinators of programs. This energy paid off well. One thing led to another. My reputation grew, until I was sought after both as a guest speaker and instructor. Also, one day a month I worked as a consultant to a small business that was hanging on a thread. Eventually, I was needed a minimum of two mornings a week. So I was quite busy."

Ramon feels very differently about his current and previous career. "I grew up in the depression and was pushed into the sales field. It was a way to avoid being on the bread lines. I paid my dues. For forty-six years, I worked for others and had a lot of stress. In the morning, I would wake up and remind myself, 'I have to get a thirty-thousand dollar sale today.' Now I am my own boss with no pressures at all. My high blood pressure is down to normal because I am so relaxed and content. The courses I teach are short enough to leave me with plenty of free time so that I can travel. My lifestyle allows me the time, if not the money, to do what I want. Social security gives me the freedom that I never had when I was concentrating upon how much I could earn. You don't really need that much money to travel. Growing older means having many elder hostels all over the place. They are very reasonable. My wife researches the costs before a trip. We generally spend very little. Being a vice president was really an ego trip. I had status, but not the recognition I get now. The work I do is very rewarding. I feel important, I am happy and I have peace of mind.

Leisure and Retirement Planning

I spoke with many others about their retirement. A large number of people felt at odds with themselves. Either they marked time by keeping overly busy or were left with too much time on their hands and not enough to do.

To avoid these extremes and find a new direction takes careful planning and commitment. Regardless of how old you are now, you are not too young to start thinking about how you want to spend your later years. Here are some hints.

1. Anticipate the stress that is generally associated with retirement.

Leaving a job when you are accustomed to working will change your life dramatically. Your self-image, leisure time, sense of belonging and financial situation are all affected. Prepare for this change by understanding and accepting its upheaval.

2. Realize that when you retire, your life is not over.

It is never too late to do anything, if you are interested enough and willing to take a risk.

3. After working for most of your life, this is the moment to actualize any fond dreams.

What have you always wanted to do? What have you been putting off until now? Assume that you still have value as a person and might want to make a contribution to the world.

4. Consider the possiblity of a second career.

You might try expanding a hobby, working as a consultant in a field with which you are familiar or continuing part-time in your present position. Draw upon the many skills you've been building over the years.

5. Go back to school for a degree or as a non-matriculated student.

Perhaps further education attracts you. Is there something that you'd like to learn more about? Let age be no barrier. When I was in college, many of my classmates were thirty and forty years my senior. The value of learning is that it keeps your mind active, widens your horizons, extends your relationships and your options. People stay young when they are mentally active and meaningfully involved.

6. Update your priorities without worrying about what others will think.

Reevaluate how your life has been spent. Your needs are important, so be positively selfish. Know what makes you happy, then try to figure out how to give yourself much more pleasure.

7. Set new goals. See what new ideas you can dream up for making life continually interesting and fun.

If you are having difficulty getting started, select one activity every day:

- that gets you up in the morning and out of the house
- that brings you pleasure
- that puts you back in your body with a new awareness; such as a massage, warm bath, cold shower, swim, tennis game or walk.
- that is related to new work or involvements

Talk to at least one stranger for about thirty seconds. You can connect with shopkeepers, mailmen, neighbors, people waiting on line at the supermarket cashier.

Be with one other person for at least a half hour daily. This person can be a lawyer, accountant, relative or a friend.

8. Stay in the moment.

Rely upon all your senses to bring you joy.

Use your eyes to examine people's faces, noticing what it is that makes each unique. As you pass familiar territory in your neighborhood, look at it as though you never saw it before.

Smell the air after a heavy rainfall, your dinner cooking, an animal's fur, the city's summer heat.

Listen to the wind, a baby crying, bacon frying, a dog barking, traffic honking, your daughter's voice as she speaks.

Taste the food that you eat, savoring each bite. Notice any subtle differences between one food and another in sweetness, saltiness or sourness.

Touch a flower, caress your daughter's cheek, stroke a kitten, hug a close friend.

Thank God that you are still alive and able to experience the world.

The senior citizens with whom I spoke all had their own suggestions for anyone considering retirement and stressed the importance of prior preparation.

- Long before you retire, decide what your options are.
- Follow your preferences and abilities and build a new framework.
- Think about what is unique about yourself, what you can offer as a service to others.

- Make lists of possible outlets to replace those provided by your job. Discover fresh approaches to investigate those ventures that seem most enticing.
- Believe that you have the right to express all of your feelings. Try not to be ashamed of screaming, yelling or crying, if that is what you need to do right now.
- Realize that you have alternatives.
- Take the initiative by being assertive and seizing opportunity when it comes.
- Be flexible, able to adapt to new circumstances.
- Forget about your age.
- Gain recognition in a new area through repeated exposure.
- Make enjoying yourself a priority.

This may be the last chapter of long life, but it is not yet time to throw in the towel. So get out there and savor every precious minute of the years you have left!

Chapter 11: Improving and Ending Relationships

Why Intimacy?

The challenge of work keeps us busy and focuses our time. But work is not a substitute for intimacy. When problems arise, knowing that someone else cares is very reassuring. People really do need people. We are sociable beings who periodically turn to each other for the affirmation and comfort of human contact. Love and mutual nurturing are strong tonics. They bring order and stability to what is often a chaotic universe. Loving another human being adds a new dimension to daily routines. Life's stresses seem manageable when they are shared.

The beginning of a close relationship is as much a turning point in your life as its ending. Both alter your perspective, self-concept and direction. Each time you open yourself to intimacy, you become changed in some way. Intimacy sometimes improves your outlook. It can make you feel elated, secure and optimistic about the future. The opposite reaction is not unusual. Some people react by being afraid or upset because they are unused to having a close relationship.

Andrew went into an emotional tailspin when he met a woman who seemed ready for closeness. Andrew was unaccustomed to intimacy. Until now, all the women he knew were unavailable. They either were married, living with someone, had a steady boyfriend or didn't like him. Rejection had become so familiar to Andrew that he had difficulty getting acclimated.

Andrew decided to explore these feelings with his new friend. They discovered that both of them experienced some degree of anxiety about their relationship. This common bond helped Andrew and his friend to feel more at ease with each other and more willing to risk further involvement.

The Loss of Love

When a loving relationship is a major part of your life, being without it is especially painful. It is not comfortable to let go of love and face your own loneliness. Even when the prospect for a reconciliation looks rather dim, most of us keep hoping.

I always find terminating intimacy difficult. I distinctly remember one affair that ended. My rage and sense of betrayal were overpowering. It took enormous psychic energy to prevent myself from destroying any positive feelings I had toward my lover. I knew that our relationship had soured and that nothing I did would bring it back to life. Nevertheless, I was determined not to give up.

This was my first experience with intense love. I loved his voice, his hands, his maleness, his arms around me and the way his mind worked. He stimulated me and challenged my thinking. It were as though he had imprinted himself indelibly onto my body and brain. The seeds of this book were planted by him, albeit unknowingly, rising from the pain, conflict and frustration into which our relationship threw me. He was my lover and muse. I felt open, stretched, loving and powerful as a result of knowing him.

I loved this man even when he held me at a distance, not wanting to get any closer. He fed my passion, cleverly fanning its flame whenever it began to abate. I felt abused, angry at him and at myself, but when I hated him I only negated myself. Because it had to end, I pushed him by asking for things I knew he could and would not give, until finally he told me that he never wanted to see me again. Our affair was really over.

When a relationship is apparently ending, how do you react? Are you willing to let go?

The way you handle the end of a relationship colors both your memories of it and later openness toward loving another person. Only when you come to terms with what happened are you really ready to form new attachments.

Nothing Ever Stays Exactly The Same

Although you may prefer that they remain the same, people and their relationships change. The status quo is often only an illusion. When put to the test over time, ties between two individuals either become stronger or gradually dissolve.

New interests, different lifestyles or a lack of proximity sometimes cause rifts between people who thought that nothing would ever interfere with their friendships. Lovers cease to communicate, turn elsewhere for solace or outgrow each other. A once passionate affair begins to erode. Friends move away, get married, divorced and have babies. They start careers, earn more money, switch professions or retire, until whatever you had in common is nonexistent.

When a relationship that's important to you isn't working, you have two options. One is to work toward building a firmer foundation, in order to salvage the relationship. The second is to leave it.

If both partners want to reestablish closeness, they must work together. This means renewing a mutual commitment, admitting their own mistakes, trying to correct them and finding ways to improve communication.

Joan, a long-time friend of mine, separated from her husband after seven and a half months. Joan and Charles argued over dividing housekeeping chores, when to entertain friends and on what to spend their money. It had gotten to the point where being together only caused further distress. The real but unexpressed issue according to Joan was that neither felt enough in control of his or her life since their marriage. Charles was unwilling to admit that he might be partially wrong. Joan knew this but was persistent. Wanting very much to keep this marriage, she learned how to control her temper by being more direct in voicing any negative feelings. Instead of keeping silent or being sarcastic, Joan clearly stated what she felt and wanted. This gave Charles the space to react and express his own needs. Communication gradually improved. Joan's changed behavior eventually made it possible for Charles to feel less threatened. He asked for a reconciliation.

Joan's attitude created an arena for a fresh start. If Joan behaves differently, so possibly will Charles. They now have a much better chance than before to work things out. I don't know if their marriage will last, but I'm betting that the odds are favorable.

Long-standing relationships are often the most difficult to change. Husbands and wives, parents and childen, brothers and sisters generally hold onto a fixed view of each other. They become so used to familiar patterns of relating that no one attempts other ways of behaving.

At work, communication tends to be even more of a problem. The work environment is rarely conducive to trust. Anxieties about losing their jobs make people jealous, fearful or suspicious of each other. However, with patience, even these relationships can be improved.

Ruby was critical and demanding of her staff. They followed her orders dilligently, but avoided any unnecessary contact with Ruby. The atmosphere was tense.

One day, when Ruby was bursting with excitement about the birth of her first grandchild, she showed a snapshot of the infant to a subordinate. The other woman's obvious pleasure in being approached made Ruby think. The next morning, she began to smile more often and to bestow praise when it was appropriate. The results were favorable. The more Ruby relaxed, the more cooperative her department became. Work improved dramatically.

Renegotiating Your Relationships

Look at the way you relate to your family, friends and colleagues. If you're not satisfied with things as they are, if you feel like you're at an impasse, try to figure out what you can do to improve the situation. Several of The Keys To Change will give you a fresh start.

Your Fantasy of the ideal relationship

Setting Goals to improve the relationship in specific ways

Time for repairing the damage and building new patterns of interaction

There are several strategies to follow.

1. Assume that it isn't ever too late to change a relationship for the better.

2. Focus on what you're doing rather than on what the other person isn't doing. Give yourself the right to feel and act as you do, giving the other person the same right. This will take the edge off your anger.

3. Realize that there are three things that you can change
   - your self-concept
   - your expectations
   - your behavior

4. Think about the specific steps you might take to remedy the situation.
   - What are your options?
   - What actions seem feasible?

5. Clear the air by verbalizing your feelings, expectations and preferences.

6. State the positive aspects of your interaction as well as its problems.

7. Cooperatively discuss possible solutions.

8. Try to drop all preconceived notions about the other person. Check yourself when you begin to react according to any present negative attitudes.

9. Be patient. Allow ample time for renegotiation.

10. Take responsibility for what you feel by speaking mainly in the first person. Make statements like "I feel," "I want," or "I don't like it when you...."

This keeps communication open.

Rather than cling to an unhealthy or unrewarding liaison, decide whether you can work together to resolve any major differences. Cooperate on a mutual course of action.

Sometimes, no matter how hard you both may try, this relationship cannot be renewed. It is then time to accept the fact that there is nothing you can do. Your relationship is over.

When A Relationship Ends

It is not easy to say goodbye to someone about whom you've cared deeply. Feelings of hurt and disappointment are to be expected, but it's not the end of the world. Try to avoid the tendency to look upon yourself as a failure.

It would be unreasonable to expect to emerge from this experience untouched, but you'll be stronger as a result of it.

I don't believe that there is much to be gained from paying attention to your destructive patterns in selecting partners, and will argue vehemently with those who do. To me, it is far more practical to try to understand your expectations, interactions and the choices they influenced. In what ways have you changed? Think about how you might apply what you've learned to future relationships.

As a review, let's look at The Keys To Change which will help you to end a relationship less painfully. They are your fear, motivation, past history of change and timing.

Your fear of this change. Since you are probably already feeling scared, give yourself permission to feel afraid. Are you anxious about being alone again, and lonely? Think about why you choose to stay in this relationship even though it makes you unhappy.

To explore this further, review the exercises Red Flags and Dark Clouds.

Your motivation for a separation. As with any change, there is also a pull in the direction of letting go. Being alone, on your own, can be very attractive.

The exercise, Green Flags, will help you to focus on your rationale for leaving. If you wish to find a balance between these pulls to leave and stay, review Embracing Opposites, Worry Beads, and Understanding Your Attitude—A Self-Test.

Your past history of change. Everyone has a record of success in coping with difficult transitions. So do you. Look back to the many instances in your life when you weathered changes, regardless of how ineptly you thought your management was at the time.

Review the exercise, Charting A Change History.

Your personal timing. The more you understand your own readiness for separating, the smoother your transition will be. There's not much point in pushing yourself too soon or too fast. Instead, review The Time Test, and Readiness: A Self-Test.

Dealing With Desertion, Separation and Divorce

Nancy cannot speak without tears of anger of the time Harvey left her and their tiny baby. "It's almost five years ago and I still cry! One day he sent a letter to me saying simply, 'I'm not ever coming back.' I felt used and angry. I was amazed at how dumb I was for loving him. His 'I love you and never want to leave you' was an outright lie! He never meant it. It hurt me that I didn't realize."

Garry, a father who recently gained custody of his children, still harbors pain and anger. He recalls the breakup: "As a brand new bachelor. I felt that I had lost everything I valued: my home, my wife, my children and most of my income for child support. For the first few days it was really tough. I felt anxious and angry, utterly powerless, with no control over my destiny. My only recourse was to grin and bear it, but that was too degrading.

My life used to be highs and lows. Now it is empty and flat. I set limits on myself because I don't want to get involved again. I prefer not to form any permanent attachments because I don't want to feel confined. Life is as usual without the headaches of a wife. My housekeeper is paid to do the same tasks and at the end of the day she goes home. But I am very angry. I was sold a phony bill of goods about marriage, and what makes it worse is that I bought it."

Cynthia is bitter about the breakup of her marriage after thirty-one years. "At the age of forty-eight, I should have more to look forward to than working the rest of my life. I am uncomfortable with seeing other people happy. I resent it." In tears now, she adds, "I ended up on the short end of the stick both financially and emotionally. I have neither the relationship nor any money. I was a good wife and so resent being alone now. I find it hard to adjust because I am man-related. When I live with, serve, zero in on a man, I feel complete. But I will not modify my behavior any more for anyone. If I did, I would slip away again. There don't seem to be a lot of choices left, so I feel sorry for myself."

Men and women in the throes of a divorce go through many painful emotions. *Accept your feelings without judging them.* Expressing your deepest feelings about this separation to a sympathetic person will help you to feel better about it. Talk to close friends who you know care about your welfare. If you can, find others who are in similar situations, and share experiences and strategies.

Sometimes couples prefer to live together for years, resigned to mutual unhappiness and a lack of fulfillment. Unwilling to admit that they either made a mistake or else grew apart, they won't consider the alternative of a divorce.

Examine your resistance to separating very carefully. Here are some typical reasons for remaining in a frustrating marriage, a review of the Red Flags exercise practiced earlier.

• "I was ashamed because I could not duplicate my parents staying together even though I knew that a future with my wife was hopeless and pointless and no compromise was possible."

• "The best relationship for a woman to be in is marriage. Everything else is secondary."

• "This is my second marriage. If I leave now, what kind of a life is left for me? I will always think of myself as a failure."

• "I put my husband through medical school and then supported him for so many years. He can't afford anything. I paid for our legal separation, but paying for the divorce on top of everything else is more than I'm willing to do. So, out of stubbornness, I won't give him this divorce."

• "I won't leave until I meet someone that I want to marry. There's really no reason to change anything yet."

- "I don't think that my wife could handle a divorce just yet."

Understand why you do want to separate, and how it can be beneficial.

When Harvey abandoned her, Nancy saw how destructive their marriage had become. "I was a warehouse for his goods. Harvey seemed to want someone to be there waiting whenever he got back. I had learned that a good woman would fetch and carry and act like a servant. But it didn't work for me. He did not appreciate my efforts to be the perfect wife. I was a marshmallow. I could have gone on forever living in the reflected glory of my husband's adventures. I was nobody on my own. I wasn't supposed to be a person.

"It wouldn't have mattered if it were just me. But I couldn't fold up and cry. My daughter was dependent upon me and it would upset her. I had to do it on my own. A whole bunch of have-to's are required with a child. With Harvey gone, I saw that I had to do something! Once I had made this commitment, I was stronger. I felt a great sense of responsibility and a fear of failing my daughter. This is what kept me going."

Cynthia also found her independence in the act of separating. "I left because I felt that I had to make a choice between the survival of my family and myself. I had stayed until then for the sake of the children. Now I knew that I had to make a decision for myself alone. The funny thing is that when I look back, I don't understand how I stayed for so long. I should have left several years earlier."

Ina has a similar story. "When I got married, I expected to live my life through my husband. The horror was that in doing this, I totally lost my own personality. We argued so much that I just gave up. I never remember saying, 'I think' or 'I feel.' We did everything his way. I became this real dependent person and made no decisions on my own. I had no outside interests then. My entire world was centered around him. I had this panicky feeling that if I let go of him, I would die. He didn't seem to feel the same way at all. The car, the furniture, the paintings, almost anything else was more important to him than I was. My ex-husband was a quiet tyrant who didn't talk to me for days. I never knew exactly what I had done wrong. I don't remember loving him and can't imagine being with him now. I am not very proud of who I was in this marriage, but of course I didn't know how to get what I wanted or needed.

"One morning I woke up and decided that if the rest of my life would be like this, I could not bear it. So it was up to me to do something. I knew that I had to leave immediately."

Nancy, Cynthia, Garry and Ina determined that their marriages hindered future happiness. Before attempting a divorce, each of them first weighed the pros and cons. Only then, when they felt truly ready, was the decision to leave carried out.

Acknowledge the importance of this relationship to you.

This attitude will free you of the past and help you to be more open to future attachments.

Deciding that it is wise to end a relationship doesn't mean that you should erase memories of your good times together. Even if there are hard feelings now, try to look back on this relationship as a positive life experience. Instead of regretting involvements when they end badly, rejoice in your capacity for loving and risking. Value yourself for having emotions, for reaching out and being vulnerable. Hopefully your next encounter will bring deeper satisfaction. Even if it doesn't, the process of taking a chance with love is well worth the effort. That's what being alive is all about!

The only way to fully protect yourself against being hurt is to close off feelings. If you play it safe, you'll be limiting yourself to a life without love. It's true that you'll avoid a certain amount of unhappiness, but you'll miss a great deal of pleasure, too.

Mourn your loss.

Take as long as you need to do this. When a union ends, the intensity of your involvement and commitment is far more relevant than its length. Assume that the greater your personal investment, the more difficult it will be for you to extricate yourself.

Old habits die hard. You may keep thinking that you hear the voice you know so well. Now no longer part of a twosome, it may be hard to live alone and think of ever loving and trusting someone again.

Being willing to let go emotionally and stand alone requires a strong survival instinct and great courage. Trust that you will gradually develop these resources and recover. To facilitate the process, review the exercises Mourning, and Mourning in a Crisis.

Looking Forward

Once you're committed to leaving, instead of looking back, focus on the present and the future. To make a smoother transition, here are a few tips.

Take responsibility for your own life.

Married or single, all you have in the world is yourself. So make yourself important. Make your own life count. This attitude is unfortunately the opposite of how many women were traditionally raised.

Cynthia says, "I keep thinking that some new man will discover me, but I know that I have to stop waiting for someone to find me and *live*."

Nancy reached a similar point. "I suddenly realized, as I stood there, on a rock pile, in a tiny cow town with the sun beating down, with no car, no husband or future and a two month old infant, that all I had were my own resources. But I wasn't helpless." She managed to slowly pull herself out of poverty, moved with her small daughter across half the country, got a job and went back to college for the degree she had never completed. Today Nancy is a systems analyst and runs a mail order business in her spare time.

Ina explains it this way: "When a relationship goes bad, there are two people in this. Don't blame yourself, but look at your own part in it. Be in a position to make a choice without letting your feelings run you. Come from being centered, strong, not needy. It took me three years and I am still learning how."

Face the future with hopefulness, confident that in time you will be all right.

Optimism will make it easier for you to start a new life. You have the opportunity to do whatever you always dreamed of doing.

Cynthia and her husband are now on very good terms. "I could always cope with life," she says proudly. "I never doubted my ability to handle anything I really wanted to do. I have pride in myself and in my work. It is certainly better for me to be out of the marriage than in it and hurting all the time. I wouldn't go back for even twenty minutes!"

Philip, whose wife deserted him and their small son several years ago says, "It never occurred to me that a man couldn't raise a child alone. I have a brain and I can solve problems. Having weathered many life crises helped me to have a positive attitude so I know I can persist."

Ina is satisfied. "My life works. I used to swallow a lot. Now I tell people what I am uncomfortable about. I have a good sense of humor that also helps. I was so ready to be different that I progressed very quickly. With fewer distractions, I can live in the moment more contentedly. I came into the world fighting too much, always twisting and turning to be acceptable to others. Now I am much more comfortable with myself. But if I had not gotten married, it would have taken me much longer to be where I am now."

Remember that sad moments never last. Life always goes on. When things are at their worst, they have nowhere to go but to get better.

Explore your preferences and options as a single person.

Update and reorder your priorities. If money is short, be practical. Tighten your belt and find new resources for income. Decide how you want to live your life.

Ina, who once thought that marriage was the only option for a woman, declares that "a career is as important as a man. If I have myself, I can be comfortable with almost anything else."

Nancy says that she is not yet ready for a serious relationship. "I want someone on *my* terms. I don't want to cater to anyone or clash wills with him. I want to look out for myself." Meanwhile, her work and family life keep Nancy busy.

Cynthia, who still feels too vulnerable to try marrying again, is continuing her career as an interior designer and planning a long distance move.

Let go of hostility and anger.

Instead of allowing yourself to feel deprived and lonely and then to blame the world for your misfortune, pamper yourself more than usual. Be self-indulgent in small ways that make you feel important. For instance, put flowers on the table for breakfast, take yourself to that fancy restaurant you always say is beyond your budget, plan a short trip for fun, dress up just to go to the corner and buy a newspaper.

If you have children, keep any hostile feelings about your ex-mate to yourself. For their sake as well as your own, don't resurrect a war which will only create additional scars.

Try to remember the good times you and your spouse had. Instead of erasing your marriage because it is over, put it into perspective.

Receive the gift of love by being open to it.

Even though you have lost someoone dear to you, do not discount what love there already is in your life. Pay attention to how many people are there for you in one way or another. Rather than pouring all your love into one relationship, or hoarding it for fear of being rejected, spread it around.

Meet new people only when you feel up to it. Be very patient with yourself about this. Just because you are not ready yet doesn't mean that you won't ever be.

Assume that you are a survivor.

The tendency to give in to despair may be very strong. When you'd like to give up this attitude, but without pushing yourself too fast too soon, make affirmative statements to counteract any anxiety you have about being alone.

When you are feeling blue and need some positive energy, there are many things you can say. Here are a few examples:

- "I am capable of taking care of myself and of doing a very good job."
- "I hurt now and miss him/her very much. But I know that this is proof of my ability to love another person. Even though it is very painful now, I am glad that I can feel my feelings and glad that I can love."
- "I have the right to feel whatever I am feeling now. I don't have to feel happy. However, I do trust that my feelings will keep changing and that eventually I will not be so sad."
- "When I am ready, I will give and receive love openly. Until then, I will allow myself to feel vulnerable. I trust that I am not too fragile to experience my vulnerability alone."
- "I count. I am important. I do not have to have someone loving me in order to believe this."
- "I am loveable regardless of whether or not someone else shares my life."

The breakup of a marriage is painful and debilitating to most people at first. In time, it is a stimulus for finding new resources, asserting your independence and planning your future. When you are able to concentrate on loving yourself, being less needy and more receptive to others, love will come from many unexpected sources. In the years ahead there will be many new beginnings.

When A Loved One Dies: How to Accept Bereavement

Suppose the one person whom you deeply love dies. If this happens, you may ask, "How can I be expected to cope with my loneliness and despair?" Life's tranquility and order have been interrupted to the extent that, unless you are deeply religious, nothing seems to make any sense.

It isn't easy, but everyone manages in his or her own way to cope. Your personal reaction to a loss, concept of appropriate behavior, habitual patterns of acknowledging or expressing feelings and willingness to ask for help are all factors relevant to your recovery.

There are several ways to accept a recent bereavement.

Examine the nature of your relationship with this person and the impact of his or her death.

Try to understand the role that this person played in your life. For example, Glenda, who had lost her daughter, said, "It was an unbearable loss. We were very close just then, with similar struggles. We had a history together. There really is no other relationship which can ever replace that of mother and daughter."

To a woman brought up traditionally, a husband is the center of her existence. When he dies, a wife with this attitude is forced to change her self-concept. Otherwise she will find bereavement untenable. All of the women with whom I talked found this readjustment of self especially difficult in the beginning.

A widow who had worked until the early years of her marriage said, "I spend my entire life doing exactly what I thought I was supposed to do. I never had permission to be anything else. My husband had died. This broke my agreement with life. After having faithfully followed all the rules, now I had no husband, no job and no life. I didn't even know who I was."

A woman of thirty explained, "I felt deserted and powerless. The only pattern of behavior clearly defined looked grim. A good widow is supposed to mourn for three years and not date. I couldn't see myself living like that."

My mother wrote about her experience, "In my relationship with my husband, I had always preferred that he be the leader. Much of the focus of my behavior was directed to winning his approval. This time in my life was like facing my own death. Without him, there was no world. My emotional clock has stopped. No longer wife, companion, sharer of joy and pain, who was I? I felt unprepared, forced out of my dependency to start a new life. I didn't know what I believed in or wanted from life."

Men voice similar sentiments about being married.

Herman's wife succumbed to Parkinson's disease after a

lengthy illness. He remarried the following Christmas, saying, "I know that it's much too soon, but I just cannot cope with being alone. The apartment is too empty with just me in it. Karen loves and needs me. I have to have someone in my life!"

Another widower said, "I immensely enjoyed being married. I still long to be part of a contributing team, to share my thoughts and feelings with someone I love. A wife would brighten my life considerably."

Look at the specific things that you have lost as a result of this person's death. Typical answers are: a sexual relationship, a business partner, someone to coddle, laugh, cry or argue with, a reason to get up in the morning, feeling needed, appreciated or cherished.

Acknowledging your loss doesn't mean that you are going to remain stuck in a position of grief. Quite the contrary. The more intensely you experience it, the sooner you will recover from your loss.

Feel all of your feelings, even the more painful ones.

Try not to censor yourself. Whatever you are feeling now is all right. Do not be concerned with the appropriateness of your feelings or with how other people will regard you if you are completely honest. Become aware of any unfinished business regarding your relationship. Until you acknowledge them, feelings of guilt, anger, sadness or relief can be a heavy burden that causes undue stress. Once they surface you will be able to express them and then let them go.

Allow yourself to fully experience your grief so that you are free of it and able to resume a normal life. There are many stages in the grieving process. Each one must be experienced. Chris, whose wife died of cancer and left him alone with their three small children, describes his own stages.

"At first I felt guilty because I never stopped her from smoking. For a year I was so devastatingly lonely that one Friday night, after the kids were asleep, I realized that I must do something immediately about my situation. So, at eleven-thirty at night, I went to a singles dance and faced about eight hundred total strangers. I felt enormous pain, but I forced myself to stand at the bar with a drink in my hand. For over two hours I stook there without talking to anyone. That evening was the beginning of an endless routine of parties and socializing. Next was a frenzy of dating and sexual encounters. Following this, I spent money excessively, rationalizing with statements like 'Life is too short. I may not be here tomorrow, so there is no reason not to buy whatever I want.' Then I realized that it wasn't important to be busy every single night. Being alone was really not the worst thing in the world. Soon, I started to settle down."

Loneliness, guilt, anger, sadness, fear, confusion about your identity or role are common reactions to death. What are your own feelings?

Love yourself now, when you need it the most.

Give yourself solace, tenderness, caring, understanding. Be good to yourself by treating yourself with as much gentleness as you would someone who was ill or hurt.

Talk to yourself softly in an inner dialogue about your recent loss and its meaning for you.

Whatever you wish someone else to do for you, do for yourself.

Seek as much solitude as you can handle in order to feel, think and plan.

Use this time to sort out your emotions, clarify priorities and take stock of what happened. Take breathing space from the hectic pace of usual activities so that you can learn more about yourself and decide how you wish to incorporate this experience into the rest of your life.

Identify the spiritual legacy bequeathed to you by the person who died.

Find something positive in his or her attitude to guide you in the future. For example, my father's legacy to me was his persistence and ability to dream. Both qualities were especially useful to me when I opted for a career change. Other possible legacies are a sense of humor, warmth, optimism, openness to change, an interest in people and the ability to stand up for one's convictions.

What special legacy was left to you?

The Keys To Change that are most applicable in cases of bereavement are *mourning, support* and *goal-setting.*

Mourning.

Give yourself the time and space to mourn properly without any pressure. Do not compare yourself to anyone else or chastise yourself for apparent slowness in getting back to normal routines. If you need a review, go back to the exercises Mourning, and Mourning In A Crisis.

Support.

Find support, but lean lightly. Reach out to people, especially those who share your loss. If they seem agreeable and able to handle pain and give you feedback, express your feelings with no compunctions. Should you feel that this is an unfair burden, there is at least one other option. Many self-help groups are organized especially for this purpose. Join an existing self-help group, or consider starting one if there are none in your immediate area.

It is healthier to ventilate than to hold in your feelings. To overcome any persisting loneliness, try to express your loving feelings toward others in words or actions.

Goal-setting.

Reevaluate your life by defining new goals to suit your current status.

First accept this death as part of your life rather than as an interruption or intrusion. You were not singled out by a vindictive God, so try not to play the victim or punish yourself for what happened. The healthy alternative to such a stance is to see what wisdom you can extract from this experience.

Use this event as a reminder of how precious life is. Think about where you'd like to be in two years. Liz, my mother, was able to learn from her changed situation.

"I came to see that I was not ready to give up, surrender or die. I was alive, with a healthy need to pick up the pieces of my life. I wanted to find a place for my energy and abilities, so as not to let the days stretch out endlessly into boredom. Life is for living, being, doing, giving, feeling."

My mother is an excellent role model for other widows to follow. She is so optimistic and assertive that I continually marvel at the rich texture of her life. At seventy-four, Liz paints, travels alone, has an executive position, pursues an active social life, swims and is close with her family. This is the same woman I worried about ten years ago on the night my father died!

Gloria is a young-looking forty-nine year-old mother of three grown children. Until her own mother's death a year ago, Gloria said that she never felt quite like an adult. "I never felt like a person in my own right. Her death was a release for me. My mother is no longer alive to tell me what to do. I was her dutiful daughter. Now I can do what I damn well please. Even though for the last twenty years I lived here with my husband, wherever my mother was seemed like my real home. But *this* is my home. My husband is here. I will be making my life with him for the rest of my years." Gloria was beginning to come to terms with the fact that, in spite of having married and raised a family, she had not previously established a separate identity.

The death of someone close can push you into looking at yourself with a fresh perspective. It stimulates you into thinking about how you might like to spend subsequent years.

The Lesson in Letting Go

Accepting the end of a relationship through divorce or death teaches you to focus on living more fully. Once the wound begins to heal, you'll reshift your priorities by asking yourself "What's important to me? What do I really care about?" Time is too valuable to waste it doing anything that has little meaning. With this outlook, you're likely to discover new interests and activities.

After his wife died, Chris became much more involved with his children.

Liz developed a wider range of friendships, became professionally involved and assumed more responsibilities.

The death of Gloria's mother convinced Gloria that she

must work more wholeheartedly at her marriage and other family ties.

What do you wish to do to make your own life count? Your updated goals may include focusing on visiting distant places, going back to school, getting a job, spending money more selfishly or less cautiously, developing greater intimacy or anything else you may fancy.

The end of an intimate relationship is either a debilitating tragedy or the begining of another cycle in life's journey. The choice is up to you.

Chapter 12: Relocating

Moving: Strain Or Gain?

For most people, moving is stressful, both physically and emotionally. Everything must be organized, packed, transported, unpacked, cleaned and reorganized. Belongings are misplaced or damaged. The household lacks order. All of this can be unsettling.

A home is more than four walls, windows and a roof to protect you from the elements. It is also a refuge, an extension of yourself and a place that provides a sense of security or stability.

Moving any distance is particularly disorienting because it requires you to leave a familiar environment and people you care about.

Anxieties usually concern
• making your new home attractive
• being accepted by others
• establishing new relationships and building a social life
• locating the people and services you need: a doctor, dentist, babysitter, housekeeper, convenient shopping center, adult education courses, etc.

Starting over in a new area gives you a clean slate. Anything is possible. How you feel is dependent upon whether your new home is an improvement and what distance you are relocating. Moves connected to any major life transition (marriage, divorce, the birth of a baby, retirement, or widowhood) require a longer adjustment period. Your first apartment symbolized independence. When your building becomes co-op and you cannot afford to remain, moving is associated with frustration. Buying a house, moving across the country, accepting a position in the next town, getting a roommate, moving in with your lover or taking a room in a hotel after a fire destroyed your home trigger many different emotions. You can clarify your feelings by posing several questions.

- How important to me are my physical surroundings?
- Is this move connected to a major change in my life?
- Does it represent an improvement in some way?
- How much choice do I have in this transaction as to if, when and where to move?

Pinpointing the source of your anxiety will alleviate it to some extent.

The Long-Distance Move

Some people have moved a great many times over considerable distance.

In the first thirteen years that they were married, Lenny and Carol moved a total of twelve times. The couple married while both were still in college. Carol, who is forty-one, spent most of the last twenty-two years raising their four children. She recently began working. Lenny is a year older.

He speaks rather matter-of-factly about their experiences. "For the most part we moved because we had to. There was no real choice about where we went. Moving is required in my profession. In the beginning, everything we owned fit in the back of a car. Later, we had more stuff and things got much more difficult. Carting it from place to place meant more logistics. After a while the kids were born. We finally took up a whole moving truck.

"I find it fairly traumatic to change jobs and to move. We had to leave deep relationships and this is always painful. I don't want to move any more if I can help it. After living here for nine years, we have established roots. I would need a much bigger incentive in money the next time."

Carol adds her own perspective. "Long-distance moving can be a nuisance, especially when the furniture doesn't arrive on schedule. I remember the time that we had to wait six weeks.

"When you go from one place to another, there is always some trauma. Some places are actually unhospitable. Once I was unbelievably unhappy. Because my husband and I are of different religions, only one family in this particular community would accept us. I don't know what we would have done without them. I couldn't adjust to the mores, had not yet learned to drive, made no real friends and so was trapped in the house with two small children. As a result of this unusual isolation, I felt as though I were on the verge of a breakdown. After two years of this, I insisted we move. Afterwards, we always researched an area before making a decision.

"Moving has enriched and enlarged my life. I feel close to so many people in so many places. Moves don't really change anything else. The structure of my life comes from taking care of my family, doing the dishes, making dinner, working at a job, making friends. The life you live is the same, no matter where you are. Life is exciting when you change your outlook, not where you are."

The long-distance move was also a positive growth experience for Elaine. Elaine is an Air Force wife. Born in the east, Simon and Elaine now live in the midwest with their three year old daughter. In fourteen years of marriage, the couple relocated four times. Within a year, they plan on moving again.

Elaine clearly remembers how hard it was in the beginning. "Our first move was from the United States to Europe. I dreamed of living abroad for so long and at last it was coming true. But I was also frightened. This was a new experience and I wasn't sure I could manage it. My mother had been sick and needed me. I needed to be with her. What right did I have to go? It was very difficult leaving my family and friends and going to a strange place where I knew no one. But I wanted to be with my husband, so I went.

"It was Hell. There was no one to talk to. I forced myself to get out so I wouldn't be alone. Otherwise I would have had a miserable time. I got a job, joined a club and met people. Since I didn't speak the language, I bought a dictionary, went into shops and practiced asking for things.

"The first separation was the hardest, but knowing that I have friends all over the U.S. and Europe is wonderful. We still keep in touch by phone, letters or visits. I've made friends I'll always have."

Elaine has a formula for getting herself settled. "The first thing I do is unpack. I organize everything. Then I put my own paintings up. My house is me. The minute anyone walks in it is evident to them that I am an artist.

"Next, I ring doorbells of neighbors who have children the same age as mine, and introduce myself. You don't make friends overnight. It is gradual. Because I play bridge and go to classes, I keep meeting people."

Elaine's experiences have given her a philosophical view of life that helps her to cope. "In order to grow and change, you have to go through things that hurt. We never have a choice of where to go. So I can either make it a good experience or a bad one. It is really up to me to make the best of things."

New Living Arrangements

Over the years you may move many times. Some moves will require greater adjustment than others, especially when they involve changes in your living arrangements. Of the following arrangements, how many have you experienced?

- Living in a dormitory
- Leaving your family to live alone
- Sharing an apartment with a roommate (or roommates)
- Moving in with a lover
- Sharing an apartment with your new husband or wife
- Living alone after a divorce
- Moving to a larger apartment to make room for a new baby or adopted child

- Living with someone who has custody of a child
- Gaining custody as a single parent of your child
- Taking care of an aging or ill relative in your home
- Living alone after being widowed, or leaving the home you shared with your spouse
- Going to a senior residence or nursing home

Living alone, with one person or many are very different experiences.

Living with someone else involves negotiation. It is important for both people to share their feelings about living together *before* taking the step. Facing the issues ahead of time will prevent many misunderstandings. Amy, who has shared apartments with others during most of her adult life, has developed a formula for determining compatibility and maintaining harmony with prospective roommates. Amy makes a list of questions that cover what points matter the most. Here are some of them.

- How much do you entertain?
- Are you a smoker or nonsmoker?
- Do your dating patterns usually include overnight guests?
- What are your preferences about sharing household expenses, food and housekeeping chores?
- What hours do you generally keep? How do you use your leisure time?

Discuss whether you expect this to be a business arrangement or the beginning of a close friendship. Even if you trust each other implicitly, financial matters need not be taken on faith. Draw up a statement concerning each person's responsibilities for the payment of rent, security, damages to property and food.

Keep communication channels open so problems can be aired as soon as they arise.

When your roommate is also your lover, employ the same strategies. Both parties share equal responsibility for the future of their relationship. Too many couples break up because they do not know how or care to work out their differences.

Even if you were married or lived with someone else before, realize that each new partner has a string of different preferences, idiosyncracies and habits that necessitate careful negotiation. Assume that your current living arrangement is a change for you and act accordingly. All the Keys To Change are relevant here (especially priorities, support, fears, motivation, fantasy, goals, planning and timing).

In the beginning, parameters need to be set for satisfying each person's needs for silence, communication, privacy, personal space and togetherness. How to spend money, share chores and make the decisions that affect both of you are major issues that must be discussed.

I suggest that you share your fears and doubts as well as your reasons for living together. Each person in an intimate relationship has a fantasy of what being together could or should be like. Since you do love each other, find the time to talk about these dreams. Mutual goals can then be set, with a plan for resolving your differences. Allow the time and space for building a harmonious and growing relationship.

Living alone may be by choice or a result of recent events. Your job may require you to live away from your family three days a week in another town. A recent bereavement or separation may mean living alone.

When Liz first became widowed, her daughters pleaded with her to move. The neighborhood was no longer safe, the house was dark and depressing and they knew that she sorely needed a change. There was nothing keeping Liz in Brooklyn except the past. But warm memories filled the rooms, making it impossible for her to consider leaving.

The daughters' worries were unnecessary. A year passed and Liz was now ready to move. She found a place in a small city that suited her, signed a lease and began a new life. Liz discovered that living alone was an experience that she enjoyed.

Living alone can be as exciting, lonely, depressing or boring as anything else. If you are used to being married or with a family, an empty house seems an unwelcome change. However, the freedom it affords you is a lovely compensation.

Here are some tips for making the most of your independence as a person who lives alone.

• Decorate your rooms so that they please you. Regardless of how long you expect to stay, make your environment seem like a home rather than temporary sleeping quarters.

• Examine your fears about living alone so that they no longer haunt you. Are you worried about being alone forever? Relax, because that's not going to happen. You do have some control over this. If, after a fair trial period, you discover that living alone is not what you want, you can always decide to share your place with a roommate or boarder.

• Balance your solitude with socializing. Chat on the telephone, invite someone over, plan ways to be with people. If you must be alone when you'd rather not be, go out for a meal in a busy restaurant.

• Consider adopting a pet. You'll feel very welcome when you're greeted at the door by a dog or cat every night. Another living presence is reassuring. If you like animals, the pleasures of owning one far outweigh the responsibilities.

• Use this time to get to know yourself a little better. Use this space in ways that make *you* happy. Indulge yourself by doing what you want to do when you want to do it. You're not accountable to anyone here.

• To ease the transition, gather support from solitude, from the furnishings you've selected and from making yourself count.

Grounding Yourself: How To Manage A Move

Moving your home can be a manageable change. The more secure you feel within yourself, the broader your perspective and the more you plan ahead, the less of a strain it will be. Focus on the following Keys to Change.

• Motivation. Know why you are moving. If it is because you're depressed and need a change, moving won't necessarily change anything but where you live. It is more likely that your problems will travel with you. If it is because your company has relocated or you were just offered a better job out-of-town, consider whether this is what you really want to do. What other options have you?

• Fear and resistance. Weigh the drawbacks against the advantages. On which side is the balance?

• Timing and readiness. Think about the best timing for this step. Are you ill, having financial problems, recently unemployed or going through a lot of stress? Try not to move your home when you are feeling especially vulnerable.

• Mourning. Before you leave your present home, say goodbye to the people about whom you care. If feasible, arrange for future visits. Visit your favorite neighborhood haunts.

• Support. If you are moving far and don't know anyone there, you can pave the way long before you pack the first carton. Get a telephone directory and look up professional, religious and social organizations with which you are affiliated. Write or call to establish a contact person. You will then know at least one individual before you arrive. The National Organization for Women, sororities, fraternities, national associations and Y's usually have local chapters.

When you actually move, be friendly. If you are less selective about whose company you are with in the beginning, you will soon get to know many people from whom to choose your friends.

If you're still uneasy, think of further preparations to put your mind at rest. Moving is one of life's challenging adventures. A final tip is one that helped Elaine to cope with all her moves. She says, "No matter where you live, that is your home."

Chapter 13:
The Loss of Health and Mobility

The Fear Of Becoming Ill

Do you ever worry about becoming physically ill and being unable to take care of yourself?

How do you react when other people are ill or hospitalized?

The attitude of some people is fairly cavalier. They breathe a sigh of relief, thinking "It will never happen to me. I'm in such excellent health that I am indestructible!"

The prospect of immobility, pain, medication, doctors, surgery or endless treatments is so frightening that it's easier not to think about it.

Suppose that normally you are a healthy, active, capable person. When you're bed-ridden for an extended period of time, life is radically different. You're no longer an independent person with a job and a steady income. At least temporarily, you're immobilized and overly dependent upon others.

The technical jargon of medical personnel is confusing. Without an adequate medical background, you probably won't understand much about the causes and cures of your physical condition. This makes you feel even more helpless. It is as though a malevolent but invisible force has invaded and weakened your body. For the moment unable to resume activities, you fear a permanent loss of function.

Convalescence in a hospital creates additional stress. Separated from those who care about you and thrust, with no preparation, into an unfamiliar and often impersonal environment, you are alone a great deal. Solitude and inactivity give you too much time to brood. This leads to your becoming overly preoccupied with symptoms and treatments. Recovery necessitates submission to the routines, timing and decisions of doctors and nurses. They, not you, appear to be in charge of your body. They, not you, alleviate pain, regulate your diet and supervise daily physical activity. Of course you feel out of control.

You may well wonder how anyone copes in this situation. Somehow they learn to live with problems they never asked for and find the strength to pursue a relatively normal life.

Facing Serious Illness

How would you manage in such a predicament? Suppose that at your next annual physical examination, the doctor announced that you were rapidly losing your eyesight. Or perhaps the diagnosis is some form of cancer, diabetes, Parkinson's or heart disease. What would your immediate reaction be?

Think about the impact of an illness upon your self-concept, work, relationships and future life-choices. An illness poses so many problems which at first seem overwhelming. It would certainly be understandable if you felt discouraged, gave into depression, hated your body or became overly self-protective. The way you react depends upon the kind of restrictions your condition imposes.

Illness raises several issues.

Being ill makes you feel different from other people.

Barry has shown considerable resistance to coming to terms with his illness. When he was only twenty, Barry began a fourteen-year battle against multiple sclerosis. Barry is dark, very thin and quite good looking in spite of a weakness in his legs that makes using a cane a necessity.

"When they first told me that I had m.s., I was in a terrible rut. I felt that I had lost everything. When I went to sleep at night, I was afraid that I would never wake up again. I hate my body. I used to be very athletic . Before this illness, I was a very involved, sociable, active person.

Now I am like an old man in many ways, unable to control my body, needing to spend a lot of time at home, resting. I am always tired.

"I want to be strong and healthy again. I feel like a freak. My illness has affected my bladder and interfered with my sexuality." Barry believes that his problems are compounded by the fact that he is a homosexual. "The gay world is hostile to anyone with a handicap. Lovers get turned off quickly or they feel sorry for me.

"This illness is so frustrating. I have all this knowledge, intelligence and creativity, but I am so anxious about my lack of energy that I don't use it. So much of my time is spent either taking care of myself or worrying about my health!"

Yet Barry has also gained from his plight. "I know that I am lucky. My upper body is not at all affected. My illness made me wiser and more compassionate toward others and appreciative of life. I became calmer and more self-reflective. I am proud that I didn't let an illness pull me down."

The problems of adjusting to an illness are caused as much by other people's reactions as your own. You are not treated like a normal person. Others' pity, scorn or overprotectiveness only reinforce your sense of isolation.

Like Barry, Irene discovered that her illness made her feel separate from the rest of the world at an age when her peers were out having a good time. Such feelings pushed Irene into making a decision which she later regretted.

Irene is a forty-seven year old divorcee who contracted tuberculosis at twenty-three when she was a nurse working with patients who had undiagnosed respiratory ailments. "For eighteen hours a day I was confined to bed although I had no symptoms and felt fine. I thought I would lose my mind. No one came to visit me because although I wasn't contagious, there is a stigma attached to TB. When I went home, I was still ostracized by my friends. At a critical point in my life, when I was still independent, everything was pulled out from under me by an illness. I was a dependent person again. Out of desperation I went back to a relationship I had broken off just before my illness. Even though I knew he was unsuitable, I married him. Although I was looking for a refuge, I didn't find one. Early on, I knew that this marriage wasn't working. Much later, I left.

"This experience taught me not to make important decisions when I am in a crisis and feeling supervulnerable. Today I take more time to think things out. My strength comes from learning to express my feelings directly when I'm shaky and from relying upon myself if no one else is around."

Coping with prolonged incapacitation requires considerable skill in relating to others. If people are to respond to you favorably, you must show them how to act by your own example. Unless you can communicate your needs, they will not be in a position to provide support.

Before her fortieth birthday, Grace was informed by her doctor that she had chronic bronchitis which required emergency surgery. Always an ambitious, hard-working articulate woman, Grace was suddenly an invalid.

"I didn't want to feel crippled. I was used to being an active person, but now I couldn't do anything without help. This was really tough because I didn't want to admit how sick I was. I was ashamed. Through it all I looked so strong that my husband never realized how weak I was. Instead of telling him, I got mad or had hysterics. Worried that I might use my illness as an excuse to be lazy, I made light of the situation. I didn't want to whine because I was afraid that people would turn away from me. Then I realized that there was a difference between complaining and informing people. I was not really being fair to people because I didn't give them enough information."

The feeling of powerlessness so prevalent during most serious illnesses is greatly increased when your diagnosis is uncertain or when you are told very little about your condition or chances for recovery. It is hard to live in the dark about what is wrong with you. More adequate information will help you cope with even the most severe disabilities.

Timothy periodically suffers from non-specific panniculitis, a rare condition about which little is known. The attacks are painful and immobilizing because Timothy's disease affects his joints.

Timothy was driving a cab and struggling to pay the bills when, at age thirty-four, he suddenly became quite ill. Hospitalization was the only logical solution. What followed was a nightmare.

"This was an extremely difficult time because no one knew what was the matter with me. I wanted them to tell me, "This is what is wrong and this is what you can do about it." Not knowing was impossible to deal with.

"Because one doctor decided that my lesions were self-induced and I couldn't prove that they weren't, I ended up in a psychiatric ward. How victimized I felt! But I was not going to give over responsibility or control and accept everything that was done to me on faith. Soon I learned as much as the doctors. They resented my questions, acting as though I were infringing on their territory.

"When they finally agreed that I was well enough mentally and physically to be discharged, I was told that I could go from hospital to hospital seeking a cure or find some other way to deal with the problem.

"Sick of being a victim, I decided to try to take charge of my life. Things started to click into place. In the beginning I had to go to work in a wheelchair. Now my attacks are less violent and frequent.

"I might have become a chronic invalid, but I didn't. Before this illness, I took a minimum of resonsibility for myself and felt out of control. Afterward, I saw that I had much more power than this. The time had come when I could make decisions about my life. I began to perceive of myself as a winner instead of a loser."

Adjusting To An Injury

Barry, Irene, Grace and Timothy were able to conquer their disabilities through persistence and courage.

A serious injury, like an illness, limits your mobility and lowers your morale. Although you may initially feel hopeless about the future, a positive attitude often reverses your prognosis.

Ellie's story is one of fierce determination. A bad fall put Ellie in the hospital for four months and kept her homebound for almost a year. The accident was only one event in a two-year series of traumas. Ellie had divorced her husband, lost her father, quit a job and changed her profession. Ellie had just started her own business when the accident occurred.

"My injuries were quite extensive. Physical therapy was necessary twice a day. This caused such excruciating pain that I thought I would lose my mind.

"When I got home from the hospital I was still in a wheelchair. I didn't know how to maneuver in my apartment or how to take care of myself. My boyfriend couldn't cope with my condition and stopped seeing me. My money was rapidly disappearing.

"I began to realize how alone I really was. When I started to cry, I couldn't seem to stop. From Friday to Tuesday, with no interruptions, I cried.

"After all these tears, I felt at peace with myself and began to pull myself together. I was very persistent and so gradually my body healed. I am finally all right.

"Obstacles seemed insurmountable to me at the time, but because I had a lot of strength and courage I was able to overcome them. I began to know myself better. There is still so much more to learn. Peeling the onion is very painful and I am still only at the top layer. But, surprisingly, after all that solitude, I now look forward to spending hours alone. I actually crave the silence. Before the accident, I saw myself as a victim. Not being very decisive, I allowed events to make decisions for me. Today my life is in my own hands!"

Recovering from an accident is similar to recovering from an illness. Both take time, patience and a growing awareness of your body. In order to get well, try to accept the weakness, pain and fragility you feel. Acknowledge your loss of health and mobility. Determine what you are able to do without causing further harm or pain. Adapt the way you move and live to any physical limitations that are necessary at present.

Realize that you probably won't be an invalid forever. It's natural to feel impatient to be back on your feet again. However, try to trust your body to heal itself in its own time. Stretch yourself a little bit further each day. Faith in the healing process can often work miracles.

When Your Condition Is Terminal

Timothy and Ellie are both proud of being survivors. But sometimes recovery is not expected. When your condition is diagnosed as terminal, coping depends upon being able to face this harsh reality without denying what is happening or giving up. How other people act now is crucial. With the support of family, friends and medical staff, the terminal patient is able both to accept death and to find the courage to go on living. In some cases, support and compassion extend a life for several weeks or months.

From the patient's perspective, whatever life remains is no longer normal. Habitual pleasures are interrupted by bouts of pain. Life seems to revolve around a variety of treatments, some of which are very unpleasant. The patient fears helplessness, unbearable pain, gradual deterioration and ultimately, death. Another problem is that the dying person is suddenly isolated emotionally from others just when support is needed most. Hospital personnel, trained to heal people, sometimes turn away because death represents a failure to them. They do not want to deal with it. Close friends and family may also be unable to handle death.

What makes them so afraid? Their fear may be less of dying than of being alive. Living is dangerous because it involves risk and involvement. Anyone who has worked with the terminally ill for any time learns that death is much less of a problem for people who took risks during their lives than for people who were cautious. For the former, the awareness of impending death helped them to savor each precious moment while they still had the chance.

The dying person benefits from knowing all the facts about this illness. It's easier to cope when others are completely honest about how they feel. Knowing that it's all right to express painful feelings and that someone will listen helps the patient to live with dignity and come to terms with death.

This kind of support is not always available in a hospital. Understaffed and overworked facilities cannot provide the humane treatment that is necessary. The patient with a favorable prognosis is more likely the one who will receive extra care. There is still a stigma associated with death. The terminally ill are carefully checked and nursed on a physical level, but unfortunately their mental health may be ignored.

The hospice movement is dedicated to solving this problem. A hospice provides the terminally ill with a quiet place to live happily and die naturally. Its interdisciplinary program consists of social, spiritual, medical and psychological services. Both hospice staff and family members care for the patient. A hospice is open seven days a week, twenty-four hours a day, so that someone is always available. Inpatient, outpatient and home care, pain management and bereavement counseling at different treatment stages are included. The accent here is on living, not dying. A hospice focuses on living life to the fullest until death.

If your condition has been diagnosed as terminal, assume that there are strategies for coping that will lessen the trauma of this episode.

• Be sure that you have acquired adequate medical information concerning your illness and its treatment. Explore the various forms of treatment that are available and the advantages of each. What risks are involved in accepting or declining treatment? Meanwhile, get a second opinion.

• Consider the merits and drawbacks of home, hospital and hospice care. Are there any special programs in your area? Check your nearest hospital, health center, clinic, counseling center, self-help group. Some hospitals are especially geared to handle the terminally ill. Should you wish more information about hospices, their design, location or how to start a program, please consult the bibliography listings at the end of this book. At this writing, more than fifteen states have hospices, with new centers developing all the time. Resources that deal with the problem of death and how to cope are also included.

• Fully examine your emotions. Have you honestly confronted and openly communicated your feelings? With whom can you discuss what is happening without denying the facts?

• Understand how this crisis has changed your relationships and direction. Now that you know that your time here may be limited, how do you want to spend the rest of it?

The Impact Of Aging

Our society is not one that respects the elderly for their knowledge or adequately provides for their needs. Instead, senior citizens tend to be segregated emotionally and undervalued professionally.

The problems associated with aging are of common concern. Everyone hopes to remain active and productive. No one wants to grow old and be without funds, in poor health, unoccupied or alone. Due to the aging process, some people become prone to illnesses. They are unable to maintain the same level of self-sufficiency as they had when they were younger. A partial solution for those unable to care for themselves is the nursing home.

Even expensive, well-staffed facilities have problems. A nursing home cannot provide the same environment or independent existence as your own apartment. Many residents feel so lonely and isolated that they believe their lives are of little value to anyone else. No longer an active member of a community, missing the comforts of home and entirely too idle, they wait for death.

Living in a nursing home does not have to be depressing.

It can be the most practical solution at certain points when no other options make sense.

Vera, a spritely seventy-six year old widow, went to a nursing home after she fell and broke her hip. Vera's optimistic attitude and determination enabled her to remain cheerful, endure a crisis and get well, in spite of her age.

"My granddaughter's wedding was in six months. I wanted to get there on my own two feet. I worked day and night. It was like a miracle. My doctor was thrilled. I don't really know what happened, because everyone had said that I would never walk again. I actually stepped down the aisle and danced at the wedding!

"Unfortunately, three days later I fell and broke the other hip. After working so hard, I was flat on my back again. But I am a determined old lady with a mind of my own. I never say, 'Poor me.' Anything I can do by myself I do, instead of asking the nurses. And I am convinced that eventually I will walk again."

Growing older does not necessarily mean having disabilities. However, should problems arise, think of Vera. Her story demonstrates how sheer will power and spunk can change even the most difficult situations.

It's a good idea to prepare years ahead so your later years are less of a burden. First take care of practical matters. Save sufficient money for emergencies, start an individual retirement account, and carry adequate health insurance. Keep yourself in good physical condition through exercise, nutrition and regular medical checkups. Broaden the scope of your life by developing hobbies and interests. Build friendships now that will last. Create the kind of lifestyle that will insure a comfortable old age.

The following suggestions are applicable to the older person as well as someone younger who are searching for ways to grow old gracefully.

• Maintain your independence. Be responsible for as many details and decisions of your life as you can physically manage.

- Find something to look forward to every day.
- Become more aware of world events. Living in the past keeps you out of the present moment and makes your company less than desirable to others.
- Reach out to others, including those less fortunate than you. Mixing with people of all ages adds texture to your social life. Instead of waiting for others to include you, take the initiative. Invite people to visit you. Since your mind is still active, use it to bring pleasure to yourself or assistance to someone else. Read more, teach a skill to a child, help a friend with a problem, converse about the things that excite you.

People want to be with those who have a zest for life. Openness to change, varied interests and an optimistic outlook will contribute to your vitality and charm. Chronological age is of little relevance because being young is mostly an attitude.

When You Are Not The Patient

Suppose your husband, wife or child has emergency surgery that warrants a long convalescence at home. Perhaps your mother (or father) will have to be placed in a nursing home or cared for at home.

When someone you care about is ill, you're likely to feel very anxious. Sickness disrupts family life, forces you to examine your relationships, threatens your ego and gives you more responsibility than you might prefer.

In each family, decisions must be made as to who will assume the burden, provide the financing and nurse the patient. This causes considerable upheaval. A husband or wife may become so involved in the other's illness that the convalescence is more stressful for the healthy partner than for the patient. If you are used to leaning on someone emotionally, you'll find it difficult to accept the fact that an illness has changed your relationship. Your "rock" or "pillar" of strength has become unusually vulnerable and dependent.

Sometimes nursing someone else reverses habitual roles

in a mutually satisfying way. Such was the case when my mother was incapacitated with her first sciatica attack. My mother enjoyed being the recipient of mothering. I enjoyed being depended upon and giving tender loving care to someone who has always given it to me.

Illness causes many feelings to emerge that are hard to handle. At times you may wish that you lived out-of-town (so no one could possibly expect anything of you now). Or you may be in the midst of a normal conversation when unexpected anger at the patient interrupts your thoughts. In spite of long and precise directions given to you by the physician, you may worry that you are making grave errors in giving medication. Physical contact with the invalid may be uncomfortable because helplessness or loss of functioning is frightening. This may be the first time that you have dealt with his or her feeding, elimination or nakedness.

It is natural to feel ambivalent, inadequate, guilty or resentful, regardless of how much or what you actually do. Even if you visit very often, you may worry that it isn't often enough. The more honest you can be with yourself about how you are reacting, the less stressful your involvement will be.

To decide what you will do to help, examine all of your feelings toward the person who is ill. Try not to censor any emotions, even those of which you may not be especially proud. Be aware of the importance of this relationship to you and how this illness has changed it. Consider very carefully how caring for the patient will affect your work, your finances, your emotional health, your time and other relationships. Then decide what responsibilities you are comfortable taking on.

Toward Recovery

Everyone who has survived a serious illness or faced dying emphasizes how the experience changed their outlook. Their unexpected solitude provided the space to explore values and reevaluate the future.

When being alive and healthy again is suddenly all that

really matters, everything else recedes. You'll have a clearer perspective about the way to get the most out of life. This is an excellent time to cherish the quiet moments of joy that you've been fortunate to experience over the years. Identify which specific activities were meaningful or challenging and which ones weren't. Then decide where you would prefer to invest your time and energy.

When you get up in the morning, spend a few minutes thinking abut how you might spend the day. Stay more in the moment by eliminating unnecessary striving, petty jealousies and stress. Savor physical sensations, ideas, feelings and conversation. Focus on what is happening here, now, in this room.

Take hold of whatever time you have left here on Earth.

Since being ill is a scary experience, articulate the things that frighten you. See whether these fears are based on reality. What can you do to alleviate each of them? Some very common fears are

1. being unable to resume your work
2. remaining an invalid indefinitely
3. being ostracized by others
4. being lonely
5. not having enough money to pay the bills
6. losing your attractiveness
7. being dependent
8. dying

What others can you add to the list?

Discussing your feelings with a friend or relative brings some relief. You will begin to see a greater number of options, even during the time you are convalescing.

Since you cannot function as you did before you became ill, during your convalescence, try to let go of the image of yourself as a physically active person with no handicaps. Acknowledge the temporary limitations you face. If you don't understand the rationale behind any physical restrictions that were suggested, ask your doctor to explain them to you.

Articulate just what it is that you either cannot or are no longer supposed to do. Is it taking long walks, swimming, playing tennis, lifting heavy packages, running, working, smoking, eating certain foods? Why are you so restricted? Be sure that you know what the consequences are of not following directions.

Then mourn these losses. Resisting only causes you greater anguish. Assume that mourning will help you to be in a position to renew these activities once again. Use mourning as a tool to get you through the recovery period and back on your feet again.

Essentially your body heals itself. Instead of resisting, allow this to happen. Recovery takes time. How long do you think it will be before you are your old self again?

Focus inward and all the answers will appear. Listen to the signals your body sends to inform you of how you are doing. It will let you know where stress persists, how hard to push, when you must rest and when you are better. While you are evaluating your progress, be extremely patient.

The right kind of support can accelerate healing. Whether psychological, financial or physical in nature, support should not make you feel too dependent. If you seek assistance, be aware of why you need it, what kind of help you wish, whom you approach and how you ask for it. You might require a ride to the doctor, someone to take a prescription to the druggist, a meal prepared or your bedding changed. Perhaps all you really are asking for is a shoulder to lean on, someone to tell you that you will be all right.

Become more aware of who you can count to be there. Some people are less able than others to deal with hospitals, doctors, pain and treatment, because they find it all too threatening. But perhaps there is another way that they can be helpful.

Know whether you enjoy being taken care of or are hesitant to be dependent. Take your feelings into account when you ask for assistance. Learn to do as much as you can by yourself, so that you feel autonomous even though you're accepting help.

What you say and how you say it will either make it easier for the other person to comply with your request or make him defensive. When one of my clients asked for help, she sounded so desperate, demanding and helpless that people turned away. To make matters worse, Marie could not take anything that was spontaneously offered, such as a helpful suggestion or compliment. She usually responded with a curt or hostile remark.

People need to be acknowledged for the assistance that they give. Try not to take what is offered for granted. If you resent being needy right now, you might consider sharing your feelings to remove the pressure. Otherwise simply saying 'Thank you. I appreciate your help' will be enough. It is quite important to receive what you are given graciously. Otherwise you will only antagonize the very people whose help you need.

How To Promote Wellness

Recovery depends upon your active involvement in the healing process. The speed and success with which your body repairs itself is directly related to your emotional attitude and cooperative role during convalescence. You'll get better faster by focusing on wellness rather than on illness.

In treating the illness as an enemy and trying to eradicate any symptoms, you will merely succeed in separating yourself from the source of life and health—your own body.

Take a more practical view. Embrace your illness and make it a part of yourself. There are no magical cures. The physician, surgeon, masseuse, physical therapist, chiropractor or acupuncturist can only help you when you take some responsibility for your illness and its treatment.

Be in your body. Acquaint yourself with bones, muscles, sinews, organs, blood and breath. Listen to the speed of your heartbeat as you tense and relax. Locate the source of your pain. Notice when it intensifies and when it disappears. Sense yourself as you breathe, move a muscle, digest your food, repair damaged cells. Trust your own recuperative powers.

There has been considerable interest recently in more holistic modes of alleviating pain and promoting healing. Instead of merely focusing on curing a physical ailment, such programs integrate the body, mind and spirit of the patient. Many of these methods involve the patient more fully in the treatment, such as visualization, meditation and laughter. The bibliography lists several resources.

To promote wellness, start with how you feel today.

1. Accept your current incapacitation.
2. Define what you can and cannot do. Then work to extend your capabilities.
3. Obtain up-to-date and understandable information regarding your condition, possible treatment and prognosis.
4. Take medical proclamations less seriously than your faith in the healing process. Believe in your ability to heal yourself—with help.
5. Listen to your body and let it set a pace.
6. Evaluate your progress periodically.
7. Maintain your independence, but ask for assistance when you need it.
8. Emphasize your right to make your own decisions about medical care and treatment after listening to the doctor who is handling your case. Get a second opinion.
9. Lead as normal a life as possible during your convalescence.

The loss of health and mobility is not your permanent status. Avoid sinking into a fit of despair by holding onto the assumption that in time you *will* get better.

Chapter 14: Wellness at Work

Symptoms of a Problem

Even though you might wish they were, not everyone is equally open to new experiences. Among your acquaintances, there is probably at least one person who makes an effort to keep things at status quo. Make a mental check of the people with whom you regularly associate. Is it your accountant, housekeeper, broker, co-worker, boss or friend who comes to mind?

One individual's inability to accept change sometimes causes problems for other people. These problems are apparent in any sizeable organization. For an organization to function optimally, people must work together in interdependent relationships. Resistance to change creates stress and disharmony.

People who resist change can be found everywhere. At a meeting, they are the ones who automatically veto all suggestions that indicate doing anything differently. In the office, they balk at every new procedure. Should you ask them to modify a word or phrase in a memo or to come in twenty minutes early one week to meet a special deadline, they immediately refuse. When trained to use more up-to-date equipment, they tend to be rather slow and unwilling learners. If the entire department is to be moved to another floor or building, for weeks beforehand you will hear their complaints. These are the ones who continually ventilate about a problem but somehow never do anything constructive to solve it. They react negatively to most new projects, ideas or suggestions.

Your inclination may be to dislike or resent anyone

behaving in this manner because of the frustration you feel. This is understandable. However, there is another way of looking at the picture.

Perversity is a way of defending oneself. It may be less painful to reject something than to admit that you're afraid of it. Try not to take people's scorn personally. Look at their behavior as a signal that they are feeling anxious. Rather than chastising them for their negativity, start to ask questions about what is causing their distress.

Where Does It Hurt?

Changes in many organizations occur so frequently and with so little preparation that it is no wonder people get upset. Let's look at the kinds of work-related changes that might cause you or your co-workers stress.

As an example, examine your own work environment. You will observe several areas where adjustment is required. If your company expands, promotes or shifts personnel frequently, staff members will face different responsibilities, surroundings or co-workers. Even when a move is positive, it may be experienced as stressful. If your boss notified you of an impending advancement, how would you feel? You might be pleased about the recognition, doubtful that you deserved it or frightened of the responsibilities and pressure that come with a new title.

Stress is also created when firms eliminate positions and terminate employees for various reasons. News travels quickly, especially when it is unpleasant. Pink slips make everyone uneasy, wondering whether they will also receive one. How secure is your present job? If you were given two-week's notice tomorrow, how would you manage?

Employee relations also cause stress. Regardless of their personal feelings, men and women are expected to work together in harmony. But habits die hard. Sexual harassment of women and few opportunities for advancement once were common practice in male-dominated firms. Today EEO regulations are aimed at eliminating flagrant discrimination. Although we have a long way to go, traditional roles are more flexible. If you are a man, it's very possible that you will be reporting to a female supervisor next month. If you are a woman, you may be the one in charge. How willing are your co-workers to adapt?

Although technological advances are useful, they require considerable adjustment. No matter how thorough your training was, current developments may make you feel professionally inadequate. If new equipment were introduced tomorrow with only a minimum of instruction, would you be able to operate it? Or would you risk surrendering your job to someone ten or twenty years your junior but much more up to date?

The Repercussions of Stress

Having to cope with perpetual changes like these can be very anxiety-provoking. The fear of being thought stupid or incompetent, of not being able to adapt, or of losing your job makes you feel very tense. When you're so busy worrying, you probably won't be performing up to par. This makes you worry about what your boss will think and what the consequences will be. It becomes an endless cycle—the more uneasy you feel, the more your work is affected.

As an employee, you are expected to leave your personal affairs at home and to concentrate upon work. As long as your responsibilities are performed satisfactorily, no one cares whether or not you are happy.

But personal problems intrude. Compartmentalization is usually impossible, especially when you are in the middle of a major change. Your work is bound to suffer the morning after you and your wife decided to divorce after twenty years together. You may be adjusting to a new marriage, the birth of your first child, the loss of your mother or trying to cope with being part of a two-career family with pre-school children.

Although psychological adjustments to change are not considered the responsibility of a profit-making organization, a high price is paid when these problems are ignored. Repercussions can be felt throughout the organization.

Morale is lowered, the rate of absenteeism increases and productivity decreases.

The Prescription: The Company As Change Agent

In your own workplace, how aware is management of these problems?

A firm with vision that wants to stay in the forefront of its competitors makes change management a high priority for all its employees. Many human resources development executives are beginning to discover that the quality of work life has a direct bearing on how efficiently work is performed. There is value in providing preventive measures, so that before a change is scheduled to occur, preparatory seminars are run.

Prime training targets are newcomers to the company, departments undergoing reorganization, employees about to be relocated, promoted, retired or terminated as well as those in management positions. For a model training program on change, refer to the appendix.

Perhaps your organization is undergoing numerous changes but no programs are being developed. You have a choice to make. Either resign yourself to working in an environment that will be stressful for some time or consider other options. If you're uncomfortable, assume that others are also. Someone has to take the initiative. Instead of passing the buck, think about what you can do to make your company more aware of the impact of change. Wellness at work requires everyone's combined efforts.

Chapter 15:
Helping Others Change

We do not exist in total isolation. Our lives touch many other lives every day. Together, we can share the stresses of today's rapidly changing environment. Each of us can do something to make it easier for someone else to cope.

Think about what involvement would be most appropriate for you. What you choose to do depends upon your interests, background, skills, personality, relationships and available time. One possibility is to actively transmit what you've learned about change. Talk about the parts of this program that made the most sense to you. Try explaining the material, even teaching someone else. This will quickly reinforce your own knowledge.

After reading this book and practicing its principles, you might wish to apply them to a social or organizational problem with which you are familiar. Or perhaps you merely want to extend greater empathy to anyone in transition whom you know or chance to meet.

Suppose that someone whom you like has come to you repeatedly for advice, suggestions, sympathy or support during a difficult period of change.

Your emotional involvement makes complete objectivity impossible. For example, you might worry that any move you make will be received badly or somehow jeopardize your relationship. If you do offer an opinion, it could be rejected or resented later. If you sit back and do nothing, you may be perceived as uncaring. Another possibility is that, feeling personally threatened by your friend's growth, you will react defensively.

Suppose that you are dissatisfied with your own responses. Can you be honest about how you feel without seeming unsupportive?

Relax, and just be yourself. In the long run, this is more supportive than trying to give someone what you think he or she needs.

The timing for a change should come from the other person, not from you. That's why it is important to listen carefully. Instead of jumping to conclusions, be sensitive to his or her needs. Perhaps a solution would be premature. People often prefer to explore their experiences and feelings with you than to look for alternatives.

If you are not clear about what to offer, merely ask. A good question is "Do you want me to listen, react or give a suggestion?" Also think about your own motivation for helping. What will *you* get from providing assistance?

All that other people really want is to know that you care enough about them to be there regardless of what they do. Your being there is a statement of interest and support. When someone is making a major change, friends often try to discourage the step. Perhaps you'll be the only person in the circle who is accepting and nonjudgmental.

This doesn't mean that you should applaud every venture indiscriminately. A good friend provides honest feedback even when it is negative. If you don't especially like the plans that are projected, say so, but gently. This sort of feedback encourages us to reevaluate our actions. Express whatever you are feeling or thinking directly. You might say, "You're important to me. I care about what happens to you. I'd like you to know that even though I won't always like what you are doing, you can count on me to support you."

Give your friends the time to discuss their fears. If it seems relevant, share your own experiences. To boost morale, reiterate all the prior changes they have made. Together explore their particular strengths and how they were able to cope.

Suggest an attitude of patience. Typically, most people lose their perspective. They worry that most of their goals will never be reached. You can say, "Hey! You look great!

And it's only been one week (or one month) since you went on this diet. I'm so proud of you!" Another tack is, "I know that you are feeling discouraged now. But let's look at how much you've accomplished in three weeks. Then we'll figure out what's left to do and how much more time you need."

You can't live other people's lives for them. Neither, in all fairness, can you tell people how to live or eliminate their problems. They have to do whatever they think is best. All you can do is watch and encourage them for making an effort.

A word of caution is necessary. Rather than becoming a crusader, rather than pushing people toward change, first check where they want to go. Otherwise you may be dictating your own goals instead of following their lead.

Be a role model for the people close to you. Your newly acquired confidence about the future and your adaptability to the present will touch everyone with whom you come into contact. This will make our world a better place in which to live and work.

Epilogue: Looking Beyond Tomorrow

We began our journey together into The Void by exploring ways to create a new and satisfying life. From there we focused on specific transition areas common to most people. Then we briefly discussed why and how to share responsibility for relieving the stress of change.

Now, your last step is to make adapting to change an integral part of your being. Practice using your new perspective as you encounter the ups and downs of everyday events. Widen your vision so that you can connect whatever is happening in your own life to a universal order.

Trust that you're capable of handling anything. Follow the flow of energy that all change generates, and rejoice in the momentum.

No one knows what tomorrow will bring. We do not have a reliable crystal ball to tell us what it is that lies ahead. Increasing shortages of fuel, housing and natural resources may make this planet uninhabitable. Computerized information banks, already a reality, are rapidly hampering your individual freedom. Perhaps next week or next year someone will discover a cure for cancer or how to resolve international disputes without gigantic loss of human lives. For all we know, Star Wars may be just around the corner.

The many possible scenarios are astounding. Experiencing them will be exciting, as long as you feel adequately prepared. But since few of us can predict the future with certainty, how can we prepare ourselves ahead of time to deal with it?

The simplest way to prevent getting caught off guard by the unexpected is to keep your eyes open and yourself in motion. Professional tennis players learn to move their feet continually and to keep their eyes on the ball so as to be ready for the next shot. Do not allow the plans you've made to control you so much that you become rigid. Being stubbornly one-tracked prevents you from veering enough off-course to ever notice the chance occurrence that could possibly turn your life around.

So stay in the present, but keep an eye toward tomorrow. Visualize yourself firmly in contact with the earth, yet indulge in frequent flights of fancy. Such a stance is not nearly as schizophrenic as it sounds. If you are well-grounded in reality, your imagination may still soar. Dichotomies can coexist within us in perfect harmony. The trick is to let them.

Our perspective is usually too narrow. In trying to be sensible and realistic, we have lost the magic. Forever earthbound, we are chained by our insistence upon having a logical explanation for everything.

A deeper sensitivity to events, people and the rhythm of life around you will help you to flow more smoothly with your environment. To me, being prepared for the future means connecting to the universe inside and outside our bodies. Being, flesh, psyche, thought, emotion and energy are one.

Use your intuition, creativity, spiritual powers, life experience and common sense to extend the realm of what is usually possible. Test the feel of "perhaps" or "yes" when considering a new direction. "No" thwarts growth by limiting opportunities.

I sincerely believe in the capacity of the human mind to effect change on a vast scale. We can transcend normal limits, reach as yet untapped potential by harnessing our collective energy. This entails intelligence, dedication, optimism, awareness, leadership, sensitivity and compassion. Be a visionary. Dare to dream. Explore the further reaches of your mind. You have an enormous reservoir of psychic energy with which to impact the universe. Anything can happen tomorrow.

Appendix
Model for a Training Program on Change

Rationale. When people are able to adapt more quickly and comfortably, the company as well as the individual benefits. Therefore it is imperative that a serious commitment be made to prepare employees for change at work, whether these changes concern the reorganization of an entire division, one department or the furniture, the introduction of a new procedure, policy or staff member.

It's always a good idea to provide as much information as possible when you're looking for cooperation. Employees must understand the rationale behind a particular change, know approximately when it will occur and how they will be affected personally. They should also know what behavior is expected of them and be given sufficient time to prepare themselves accordingly.

Case studies for the sessions should be based upon the specific problems and situations of seminar participants, both at home and on the job.

Sample situation. A firm expects to hire ten women managers within the next two months, as a result of EEO requirements.

Program content.

• *Get a historical perspective.* Focus on any past events which seem relevant to the present situation. Discuss the ratio of male and female employees in the previous ten years and the kinds of jobs women have held. Then compare the projected number of women to be hired this year. Give the rationale behind the change. Research what other similar companies are doing regarding promoting or hiring women. Learn how new female employees were received. Consult representatives from firms that implemented this change for strategies and suggestions.

• *Understand timing factors and expand employees' readiness.* Discuss the projected time plan for hiring women in terms of the readiness of the various department staff to accept them.

• *Be more aware of employees' resistance.* First identify what resistance exists. If the company will be greatly reorganized to accomplish this shift in personnel, consider which positions will be affected the most. Explore the participants' attitudes toward working with women. Have them state both the advantages and the problems they anticipate. Estimate the forms that antagonism would take, such as silence, jeering, sexual innuendoes. Allow employees the chance to express their negative feelings without recrimination and to discuss ways of resolving them.

• *Set goals and prepare plans.* Figure out what will facilitate this change. Enlist the assistance of as many people as possible in planning, especially the departments directly affected. Develop a step-by-step strategy, as well as alternate plans.

• *Gain support within the organization.* A change is most effective when those in positions of power endorse it. Discuss the expectations of top management. Do they merely give lip service to EEO regulations, but secretly hope that the project will be sabotaged? Or do they sincerely want women to be successful? Ask the group if all employees were informed about the added positions. Some staff members will be more receptive than others. Identify them and utilize their support.

Look at what has already been done to prepare for this change. What steps were taken, with what results? Consider which problems or details have not yet been worked out.

Provide the space for exchanging ideas. You might call in key people in the firm's top positions who are the most flexible and the least threatened by women in power. Or send a memo asking for ideas from the staff on how to ease this transition period. Team-building brings people together in a spirit of cooperation so they will be more receptive to and less threatened by change.

• *Take immediate action.* Start as soon as possible to implement the ideas which were just developed in the planning sessions. Evaluate the project's effectiveness at each stage. Use these evaluations to suggest modifications of the plan.

Selected Readings and Resources

Change (General):

Abell, Richard, M.D. *Own Your Own Life*. New York: Berkley Publishing Corporation, 1979.

Delaney, Gayle. *Living Your Dreams*. New York: Harper and Row, 19.

Dyer, Wayne W., Dr. *Your Erroneous Zones*. New York: Avon, 1976.

———. *Pulling Your Own Strings*. New York: Crowell, 1978.

Ferguson, Marilyn. *The Aquarian Conspiracy: Personal and Social Transformation in the 1980's*. Los Angeles: J.P. Tarcher, 1980.

Flach, Frederick. *Choices: Coping Creatively With Personal Change*. New York: Bantam, 1979.

Garfield, Patricia, Ph.D. *Creative Dreaming*. New York: Ballantine, 1974.

Gould, Roger L., M.D. *Transformations: Growth and Change in Adult Life*. New York: Simon and Schuster, 1978.

Grossman, Lee. *The Change Agent*. New York: Amacom, 1974.

Harris, Dr. Philip R. *Effective Management of Change: Supplemental Instructional Manual*. Pittsburgh: Westinghouse Learning Corporation Training Systems Division, 1974.

Heller, Robert. *Super Self: The Art and Science of Self-Management*. New York: Atheneum, 1975.

Jacobs, Dorri. *Priorities: How to Stay Young and Keep Growing*. New York: Franklin Watts, 1978.

Johnson, Wendell with Moellar, Dorothy. *Living with Change: The Semantics of Coping*. New York: Harper and Row, 1972.

Marris, Peter. *Loss and Change*. New York: Anchor, 1975.

Miller, Gordon Porter. *Life Choices: How to Make the Critical Decisions about Your Education, Career, Marriage, Family, Lifestyle*. New York: Crowell, 1978.

Osborne, Christopher E. J. *Towards a Model of Individual*

Response to Rapid Change. U. of Lancaster, U.K., Master's thesis, 1980. Available through Box 96, Trinity Pass, Pound Ridge, New York 10576.

Otto, Herbert. *Group Methods to Actualize Human Potential: A Handbook.* Beverly Hills: Holistic Press, 1970.

Reeshel, Gerald, Dr. *Centering: Six Steps toward Inner Liberation.* New York: Times Books, 1979.

Sheehy, Gail. *Passages: Predictable Crisis of Adult Life.* New York: Bantam, 1977.

Sher, Barbara, with Gottlieb, Annie. *Wishcraft: How to Get What You Really Want.* New York: Viking, 1979.

Toffler, Alvin. *Future Shock.* New York: Bantam, 1970.

——. *The Third Wave.* New York: William Morrow, 1980.

Viscott, David, M.D. *Risking.* New York: Pocket Books, 1977.

Weinberg, George, Dr. *Self-Creation.* New York: Avon, 1978.

Wheelis, Allen. *How People Change.* New York: Harper Colophon Books, 1973.

Resources: National Self-Help Clearing House. Alan Gartner and Frank Riessman, Co-Directors. C.U.N.Y. Graduate School and University Center, 33 West 42 Street, New York, New York 10036. 212-840-7606.

An organization that publishes a directory of self-help groups, provides information of starting your own group. Groups in existence include issues related to: specific diseases, tenant power, consumerism, widows, mentally ill, child abuse, divorced, new parents, parental stress, etc.

World Future Society. 4916 St. Elmo Avenue, Washington, D.C. 20014.

An interdisciplinary association of individuals interested in the future. Services include publications, meetings, local chapters, bimonthly journal, conferences, book service.

Crisis, Depression:

DeRosis, Helen A., M.D. and Pellegrino, Victoria Y. *The Book of Hope: How Women Can Overcome Depression.* New York: MacMillan, 1976.

Feinberg, Dr. Mortimer R., Feinberg, Gloria and Tarrant, John J. *Leavetaking: How to Successfully Handle Life's Most Difficult Crises.* New York: Simon and Schuster, 1978.

Goodman, Ellen. *Turning Points: How People Change, through Crisis and Commitment.* New York: Doubleday, 1979.

Gordon, Barbara. *I'm Dancing As Fast As I Can.* New York: Bantam, 1979.

Kliman, Ann S. *Crisis: Psychological First Aid for Recovery and Growth.* New York: Holt, Rinehart and Winston, 1978.

Morris, Sarah, Ph.D. *Coping with Crisis.* Chicago: Chicago Review Press, 1978.

Moustakas, Clark E. *Loneliness.* Englewood Cliffs: Prentice-Hall, 1961.

_____. *Turning Points.* Englewood Cliffs: Prentice-Hall, 1977.

Selye, Hans. *The Stress of Life.* New York: McGraw-Hill, 1956.

Resources: Women In Crisis Annual National Conference. Jane Velez, Director. 37 Union Square West, New York, New York 10003 212-242-3081.

Unemployment, Career and Job Change, Money:

Bolles, Richard Nelson. *The Three Boxes of Life: An Introduction to Life/Work Planning.* Berkeley: Ten Speed Press, 1978.

_____. *What Color Is Your Parachute? A Practical Manual for Job Hunters and Career Changers.* Berkeley: Ten Speed Press, 1972.

Figler, Howard. *The Complete Job Search Handbook.* New York: Holt, Rinehart and Winston, 1979.

Gallagher, James. *The Manager's Guide to Outplacement.* Career Programs Press, 60 East 42 Street, New York 10065, 1981.

Gillies, Jerry. *Moneylove: How to Get the Money You Deserve for Whatever You Want.* New York: Warner, 1978.

Jeffers, Susan J. and Carr, Ellen F. *How to Find a Job: A Woman's Handbook.* New York: Jeffers/Carr Associates, 307 E. 44 Street, New York 10017, 1980.

Laut, Phil. *Money Is My Friend.* Chaula Vista, California: Trinity Press, 1978.

New Vocations Project. *Working Loose.* San Francisco: American Friends Service Committee, 1971. Distributed by Random House, Inc., New York.

Stetson, Damon. *Starting Over.* New York: MacMillan, 1971.

Resources: Catalyst. 14 East 60 Street, New York, New York 10022. 212-759-9700

A national non-profit organization that helps women choose, launch and advance their careers. Offers career information and guidance through a network of women's resource centers.

The Human Economy Center, P.O. Box 551, Amherst, Massachusetts 01004.

A network of people sharing information, values and ideas concerning alternatives to the large-scale market economy. Includes new approaches to work organization, health care, education, energy, creativity, economics.

Workshare, c/o Patricia Lee Associates, 311 East 50 Street, New York, New York 10022. 212-832-7061

A member-based resource center for job-sharing opportunities.

Retirement And Aging:
Bradford, Leland P. and Martha I. *Coping with the Emotional Upheavals of Retirement.* Chicago: Nelso Hall, 1979.

Dangott, Lillian R. and Kalish, Richard. *The Pleasures of Aging.* Englewood Cliffs: Prentice Hall, 1979.

Downs, Hugh and Roll Richard. *The Best Years Book: How to Plan for Fulfillment, Security and Happiness in the Retirement Years.* New York: Delacourt Press, 1980.

Otte, Elmer. *Retirement Rehearsal Guidebook: A Helpful Planning Guide for the Retirement Task You Must Do for Yourself.* Pictorial, Inc. 1718 Lafayette Rd., Indianapolis, Indiana, 46222.

Preuss, Karen, with Henkin, William. *Life Time: A New Image of Aging.* Santa Cruz: Unity Press, 1978.

Seskin, Jane. *More Than Mere Survival: Conversations with Women Over Sixty-Five.* New York: Newsweek, 1980.

Changing Relationships, Marriage, Divorce:
Bach, George and Deutsch, Ronald. *Pairing: How to Achieve Genuine Intimacy.* New York: Avon, 1970.

Bach, George and Wyden, Peter. *The Intimate Enemy.* New York: Morrow, 1968.

Bengis, Ingrid. *Combat in the Errogenous Zone.* New York: Bantam, 1973.

Fromm, Erich. *The Art of Loving.* New York: Harper and Row, 1956.

Gittleman, Susan and Markowitz, Janet. *The Courage to Divorce.* New York: Ballantine, 1974.

Krantzler, Mel. *Creative Divorce: A New Opportunity for Personal Growth.* New York: Signet, 1973.

O'Neill, George and Nena. *Open Marriage.* New York: M. Evans and Company, 1972.

_____. *Shifting Gears: Finding Security In a Changing World.* New York: M. Evans and Company, 1974.

Otto, Herbert, ed. *Love Today: A New Exploration.* New York: Association Press, 1972.

Peele, Stanton and Brodsky, Archie. *Love And Addiction.* New York: Signet, 1976.
Pietsch, William. *Human Be-Ing: How to Have a Creative Relationship Instead of A Power Struggle.* New York: Signet, 1975.
Stevens, Barry. *Don't Push the River.* Lafayette: Real People Press, 1970.

Death, Dying And Bereavement:
Becker, Ernest. *The Denial of Death.* New York: Free Press, 1973
Burgess, Jan and Kohn, Willard. *The Widower.* New York: Beacon, 1978.
Caine, Lynn. *Widow.* New York: Bantam, 1975.
Cohen, Kenneth. *Hospice: Prescription for Terminal Care.* London: Aspen Systems Corporation, 1979.
Hendin, David. *Death As a Fact of Life.* New York: Warner, 1974.
Jury, Mark and Dan. *Gramp: A Man Ages and Dies.* New York: Grossman, 1976.
Kubler-Ross, Elizabeth. *Death, The Final Stage of Growth.* Englewood Cliffs: Prentice-Hall, 1975.
_____. *On Death and Dying.* New York: MacMillan, 1962.
_____. *Questions and Answers on Death and Dying.* New York: Warner, 1974.
_____. *To Live Until We Say Goodbye.* Englewood Cliffs: Prentice-Hall, 1978.
Lear, Martha. *Heart Sounds.* New York: Simon and Schuster, 1980.
Stoddard, S. *The Hospice Movement: A Better Way of Caring for the Dying.* New York: Vintage Books, 1978.

Resources: To locate the nearest hospice, contact The National Hospice Organization, 765 Prospect Street, New Haven, Connecticut 06511, 203-789-1509.

Thanatology Foundation, Dr. Austin H. Kutscher, President, 630 West 168 Street, New York, New York 10032. An organization to reeducate students and professionals who provide services to the bereaved. Publishes books, provides referral service and symposia on grief, bereavement and disease.

The Society of Compassionate Friends, Main Office: P.O. Box 1347, Oakbrook, Illinois. Local support groups for bereaved parents.

Highly Specialized Promotions, 391 Atlantic Avenue, Brooklyn, New York 11217. Tel. 212-UL-8-3026. Collection of books and audio-visual materials on death, bereavement, loss and grief.

Illness And Wellness:
Bresler, Dr. David E., with Trubo, Richard. *Free Yourself from Pain.* New York: Simon and Schuster, 1979.
Cousins, Norman. *Anatomy of an Illness.* New York: Norton, 1979.
Grollman, Earl A. and S. *Caring for Your Aged Parents.* New York: Beacon, 1978.
Olshan, Neil H. *Power Over Your Pain without Drugs.* New York: Rawson, Wade, 1980.
Oyle, Irving, M.D. *The Healing Mind.* Milbrae, California: Celestial Arts, 1979.
_____. *The New American Medicine Show.* Santa Cruz: Unity Press, 1979.
Routh, Thomas A. *Choosing A Nursing Home.* Springfield: Charles C. Thomas, 1970.
Simonton, O. Carl, M.D., Matthews-Simonton, Stephanie, and Creighton, James. *Getting Well Again: A Step-By-Step Self-Help Guide to Overcoming Cancer for Patients and Their Families.* Los Angeles: J. P. Tarcher, 1978.
Wallace, Amy and Henkin, Bill. *The Psychic Healing Book.* New York: Dell, 1978.
Resources: Film: Coping with Serious Illness. Time Life Video, 1980. Contact U. of Illinois Film Center, 1325 S. Oak Street, Champaign, Illinois 61820.

Dorri Jacobs, Ed.D., is the director of Programs On Change, a firm which offers lectures, consulting, training and counseling services to industry, groups and individuals. The firm's specialties are managing change in careers, relocation, the work environment, retirement and lifestyle, stress reduction, team-building, creative time management and procrastination. Her private practice includes groups for people in transition and for professionals in the arts.

Currently on the faculty of the YWCA Women's Center in New York, Dr. Jacobs has taught at The New School for Social Research, Queensborough Community College, the University of Bridgeport and Fairleigh Dickinson University. A former consultant for The New York State Council on the Arts and The Leonard Davis Center for the Performing Arts, she has presented programs for numerous organizations. These include Abraham & Straus, The American Society for Training and Development, The American Association of Artist-Therapists, Inc., The Association for Humanistic Psychology, The American Dance Guild, Inc., The Career Development Specialists Group of New York, The City University of New York, Lord & Taylor, Montclair State College, The National Art Education Association, The National Council of Jewish Women, The National Organization for Women, The New York Society for General Semantics, New York University, Parents without Partners, The Port Authority of New York, The Social Security Administration and the YWCA.

Her articles have appeared in *New Woman* and *Family Circle* Magazines and many professional newsletters. She is active in the fields of psychology, business, education and the arts and a member of several professional organizations.

Dorri Jacobs is the author of a previous book, *Priorities*.

Your feedback on *Change: How to Live with, Manage, Create and Enjoy It* is requested. Please send your comments to Programs On Change, Suite 1-C, 784 Columbus Avenue, New York, N.Y. 10025.